Other Titles by Vermilion:

The Six Value Medals

How to have a Beautiful Mind

How to have Creative Ideas

Think!

Six Frames

Serious Creativity

Lateral Thinking

The Mechanism of Mind

H + (Plus) A New Religion?

PARALLEL THINKING

FROM SOCRATIC THINKING TO DE BONO THINKING

Edward de Bono

Vermilion
LONDON

1 3 5 7 9 10 8 6 4 2

Vermilion, an imprint of Ebury Publishing,
20 Vauxhall Bridge Road,
London SW1V 2SA

Vermilion is part of the Penguin Random House group of companies
whose addresses can be found at global.penguinrandomhouse.com

Penguin
Random House
UK

Copyright © McQuaig Group Inc., 1994
Drawings copyright © Peter Caspar, 1994

Edward de Bono has asserted his right to be identified as the author of this
Work in accordance with the Copyright, Designs and Patents Act 1988

Published with permission from de Bono Global Pty Ltd
www.debono.com

This edition first published in the United Kingdom by Vermilion in 2016
First published by Viking in 1994

www.penguin.co.uk

A CIP catalogue record for this book is available from the British Library

ISBN 9781785040856

Printed and bound in Great Britain by Clays Ltd, St Ives PLC

Penguin Random House is committed to a sustainable future for our business,
our readers and our planet. This book is made from Forest Stewardship
Council® certified paper.

MIX
Paper from
responsible sources
FSC
www.fsc.org   FSC® C018179

CONTENTS

PREFACE

I want to make it clear at the outset that it is not my intention to demonstrate that Western thinking is bad and that Eastern thinking is good. Eastern thinking, if there is such a collective entity, does not come into this book except occasionally and indirectly. The contrast I wish to highlight is between traditional Western thinking with its judgemental and adversarial habits and 'parallel' thinking with its emphasis on possibility and designing a way forward.

My intention is to show that, in a changing world, Western thinking is failing. It is failing not because it is being applied ineffectively but because there are deep-seated inadequacies and dangers in the system itself.

Western thinking is failing because it was not designed to deal with change.

Does this mean that the traditional Western thinking system that was fashioned by what I refer to as the Greek Gang of Three (Socrates, Plato and Aristotle) was wrong? To answer with a simple 'Yes' or 'No' would be to use the judicial terminology of the system itself. Western thinking is failing because it was not designed to deal with change. The main fault is the esteem, reverence and complacency with which we have allowed ourselves to be satisfied with an inadequate system.

Digging for gold is not the same as designing and building a house. Analysis and judgement are not enough when there is a need to design a way forward.

The purpose of this book

It is not my intention simply to point out the limitations and faults of the traditional system. That, again, would be to use the habits of that system. I intend to lay out the nature and operating methods of a different thinking system. This is 'parallel' thinking. In this method, instead of using the boxes and judgements of traditional thinking, we 'design forward from a field of parallel possibilities'. I hope to make clear that this is a fundamentally different method of thinking.

Parallel thinking is more concerned with 'what can be' than with 'what is'.

If you want to know what I hope to achieve in this book then you could turn to my conclusions in the summaries on pages 255–68.

If you have been educated entirely within the traditional Western thinking system devised by the Gang of Three, that thinking system will appear complete, comprehensive and perfect. You will see the world through the belief system that underlies that system. You will argue about the world using the devices provided by that system.

Yet in a rapidly changing world the traditional thinking system is failing because it was never designed to deal with change. The system is inadequate. It is dangerous. It is complacent.

This is a book not about philosophy but about the practical operation of thinking. It is my intention to compare the traditional Western thinking system with 'parallel' thinking. There are some very fundamental points of difference.

Traditional thinking is concerned with search and discovery. Parallel thinking is concerned with design and creation.

Traditional thinking is based on ruthless and immediate judgement (yes/no, right/wrong, true/false). Parallel thinking accepts 'possibilities' without judging them.

Traditional thinking is concerned with 'rock logic' and 'is'. Parallel thinking uses the flow of 'water logic' and 'to'.

Traditional thinking uses hard-edged judgement boxes, definitions and categories. Parallel thinking uses soft edges, overlap, flagpoles and spectra.

Traditional thinking sets up dichotomies and contradictions in order to force a choice. Parallel thinking embraces both sides of a contradiction and seeks to design a way forward.

Traditional thinking believes that information and judgement are enough. Parallel thinking looks to the deliberate generation of ideas and concepts.

Traditional thinking overuses criticism in the belief that if you remove 'bad things' then what is left will be wonderful. Parallel thinking sets out to construct 'wonderful' things.

Traditional thinking uses adversarial argument and refutation to explore a subject. Parallel thinking uses cooperative 'parallel' thinking.

I shall attempt to make the differences very clear. Sometimes there are fundamental differences between the two methods. Sometimes it is more a matter of degree and of emphasis. Anyone on the surface of the globe is either equidistant from the North and South Poles or nearer one than the other.

What is important in reading through the book is to note the differences. You will get the most value from the book if you focus on these differences. If, because of your education and background, you read through the book in a defensive frame of mind and seek to defend traditional thinking at every point then you will be wasting your time. You will see only the overlap and none of the key differences.

Traditional thinking is concerned with search and discovery. Parallel thinking is concerned with design and creation.

One of the values of the comparison between traditional Western thinking and parallel thinking is that the reader is forced to look at the peculiar nature of Western thinking. Usually this is difficult because we are so trapped inside this system that we cannot get outside to look at it objectively.

Parallel thinking is a practical thinking system. In different ways it is already in use and has been for some years. Throughout this book I refer to some of the practical techniques which can be studied and used.

The essence of parallel thinking is to move forward from possibilities, in contrast to exercising judgement at every moment. That is the way this book should be read; exercise your judgement at the end.

I shall be referring to 'traditional Western thinking', 'the traditional system', 'the Gang of Three' and 'the Socratic method' somewhat interchangeably, since there is no single term with which to refer to our traditional thinking system. At the beginning of the book I shall attempt to show why and how this particular type of thinking system was set up and why it came to dominate Western civilization. The system has many strong virtues and a high usefulness, and yet there are reasons why it is failing today.

Just as this is not a book on philosophy, it is not a book on history. So do not waste your reading time quibbling and nitpicking, because this may well interfere with your understanding of the difference between parallel thinking and our usual method.

At the end of the book you should be able to say: 'I can see that there is a clear difference between whisky and vodka – even though there is alcohol in both. I prefer whisky to vodka. Or, there are times when I prefer whisky and times when I prefer vodka.' If you cannot do that then the blame may be equally divided between the writer of this book and the reader.

1 THE WRONG TACKLE

Have you ever gone fishing and taken the wrong bait and the wrong tackle?

If you know that you have the wrong bait and the wrong tackle then you are frustrated by knowing at every moment that you could be doing rather better than you are doing. You think to yourself: 'If only I had brought the right equipment things would be so much easier and so much more successful.'

But what if you do not know that you have the wrong bait and the wrong tackle? It will just seem to you that catching fish at that place or time is very hard indeed. It will not occur to you to blame your equipment. Suppose you are not aware of any alternative equipment. The bait and tackle you have with you are the only ones available. Everyone uses them. Everyone finds that catching fish is rather hard. That is accepted. Why should you expect someone to come along and to suggest different bait or tackle? At best you blame yourself that your skill with the standard bait and tackle is not as high as it should be. If you were to complain to anyone about the difficulty of catching fish, you would be told to fish 'properly' and to develop more skill with the standard equipment.

Just suppose that our standard 'thinking equipment' is the only one we know. If we are not 'catching enough fish' then we need to develop more skill in using this standard equipment. Can we conceive, however, that there might be 'better

1

equipment'? Can we conceive that our standard, traditional thinking methods are not the only ones and perhaps not the most appropriate ones? Fishing equipment has improved considerably over the ages. Has our thinking equipment also improved, or are we still proud to be using the equipment designed about 2,500 years ago?

We can take the complacent view and declare that our thinking methods are pretty good because we have made a lot of progress in science and technology and raised the living standards of some of the world's population. Our behaviour and values are also considerably less 'barbaric' than they used to be. Many countries have abolished the death penalty, and some have almost abolished smoking.

We can take the complacent view that poverty, pollution, local wars and local chaos are the inevitable result of change and of human nature. Such things will always happen, and we are getting more competent in dealing with them, just as we have become much more conscious about ecology. There is not much wrong with this complacent view, and it has the merit of defending itself vigorously and well.

If, however, we were to have doubts about this complacency (doubting complacency is a classic oxymoron) then we might get around to asking ourselves three possible questions:

1. Is it possible that some of our troubles are actually caused by inadequate thinking habits?
2. Is it possible that our difficulty, and sometimes inability, to put things right is due to inadequate thinking methods?
3. Is it possible that better thinking could make things better?

Here the analogy of the fisherman breaks down. Many fishermen would be eager to try out new tackle and new bait. Not so with thinking, where we are wedded to and bedded down in traditional thinking habits.

Is it possible that our difficulty, and sometimes inability, to put things right is due to inadequate thinking methods?

At a time of rather rapid change there is perhaps a higher demand for thinking that is more constructive, more creative and more effective. This obviously applies to global issues but it also applies to matters that are the concern of nations, communities, families and selves. World peace is a worthy objective, but so is personal peace.

The standard traditional Western thinking style was set by the famous Greek Gang of Three: Socrates, Plato and Aristotle. Their contribution was astounding, but it may be time to move on. The traditional style of thinking set by this Gang of Three may not be fully adequate to cope with the demands of the increasing complexity of a rapidly changing world. In this book I intend to examine the adequacy of our hallowed thinking habits. The purpose is not merely to criticize, which is an easy exercise of intellect, but to suggest alternatives in those places where the traditional method seems inadequate.

2 ORDER OUT OF CHAOS

Figure 1 overleaf shows a random assembly of dots which are probably mature enough to be called blobs.

You can look at each blob on its own or you can start grouping the blobs together. You can group blobs that seem to form neighbourhood groups or you may have in mind some formal number for a group and then seek out ways of grouping the blobs in threes or fours.

You can choose to look at the blobs as you like. It is a matter of personal perception and choice. Perception is always a matter of choice, even if the choice has been made for us by our experience or education or by the emotion of the moment. The great sophist* Protagoras was all for perception. He maintained that the world was as each person chose to see it. His famous saying, 'Man is the measure of all things', expressed this rather individual version of truth. All perceptions were equally true. God existed for those who wanted to believe in God.

Obviously, this highly personal view of truth was messy and chaotic, and it could be manipulated by the skilled teachers of rhetoric who gave paid classes in 'persuasion' and the methods of changing people's view of the world.

Then came Socrates followed by Plato and they created order out of chaos by making truth 'absolute'.

* A sophist was a paid teacher of philosophy, rhetoric and persuasion in Greece in the classical period.

Figure 1

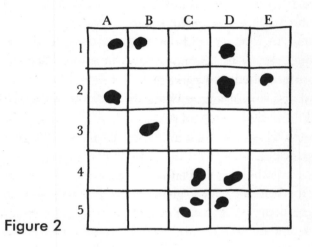

Figure 2

Look now at Figure 2. The imposition of the grid means that each blob now has a fixed position and name. A blob is now A2 or C4. Even if we do choose to group things differently from time to time, there is an underlying 'truth'.

For the moment we do not need to worry about whether the order has been imposed on the chaos or discovered in the chaos. The important thing is that there is now order.

Socrates followed by Plato created order out of chaos by making truth 'absolute'.

6

3 ORDER

Plato is rightly regarded as the father of Western thinking. He gave civilization a powerful thinking method.

Plato was an out-and-out fascist. But he was a good guy who meant well and did not seek any power for himself, so you are not supposed to suggest such things.

It is not surprising that Western thinking has been intrinsically fascist in nature, with rigid rules, harsh judgements, inclusion and exclusion, category boxes and judgements, and a high degree of righteousness.

In his *The Republic*, Plato suggests that society is to be ruled by a special class called 'guardians'. These are originally to be soldiers, who then take over government. They in turn are divided into the 'rulers', who make policy decisions, and the 'auxiliaries' (police, etc.), who carry out the policies. Ordinary people are to have no say in government whatsoever – but of course the enlightened rulers have been properly educated to look after the interests of ordinary people.

The guardians are a sort of hereditary caste who are to be bred on strictly scientific lines, just as the best racehorses might be bred or the Germans sought to produce pure Aryans. Families and private wealth are distractions and are to be abolished. There are to be State nurseries for children, so women will be relieved of domestic slavery.

The State is to come first, and people have to fit in with the interests and needs of the State. There is to be censorship in the arts and in the material allowed into education. Nothing that might threaten the State is to be permitted. The whole purpose of education is to produce a small elite of guardians. Breeding is to be arranged through special marriage festivals.

It is not surprising that the Nazi Party in Germany had as one of its official aims the 'production of Guardians of the highest Platonic ideals'. It is also not surprising that there are strong echoes of Plato in the Marxist approach to State and government. As Sir Karl Popper put it: 'The criterion of morality is the interest of the State. Morality is nothing but political hygiene.'

In his work *Gorgias*, Plato puts forward a bully-boy type of fascist who believes that might is right and that the better and more powerful should rule. In *The Republic*, Thrasymachus claims that morality is only the self-interest of the 'stronger'. Both these people are presented in order to be refuted. Plato was not advocating bully-boy fascism and was against the rule of wealth. What he wanted was competence.

Critias was the cousin of Plato's mother, Perictione. After the defeat of Athens by Sparta in 404 BCE a commission of 30 was set up to draft a new constitution. These soon became the 'Thirty Tyrants', who seemed to have exploited power for their own purposes. Critias was one of the Thirty Tyrants, yet Plato never seemed to criticize Critias.

Western thinking is thoroughly fascist in its righteousness and certainty.

Plato and Critias were in agreement that uncontrolled democracy was the ruin of the State – as it had indeed been in Athens. Democracy in Athens was rather different from democracy today. Women, slaves and people born in other cities did not vote. Everyone else met in the Assembly to vote on matters. Voting was direct; there were no intervening representatives. Plato believed that this was dangerous, because people's views could easily be swayed – just as there are fears today that skilled and professional electioneering can control election outcomes.

At the same time, the sophists were running schools of rhetoric which were precisely aimed at developing the skills of persuasion and claimed that with such skills 'the weak argument could be made the stronger'. The sophists were also relativists and doubters. They believed in expediency and the dominance of the perceptions of the moment.

So, faced with a 'rabble' democracy and the development of unscrupulous skilled persuaders, Plato opted for a government of competence based on rulers who had been bred and trained to rule.

Because Plato was a fascist does not mean that we ought to exercise the sort of category judgement of him which traditional thinking demands. We could call him a centralist, a totalitarian, an authoritarian or, simply, a Utopian.

Plato was concerned with order, rules, truth, absolutes, and the boxes and principles which allow the exercise of clear conscious judgement. This style applies equally to the imposition of fascist order in a State and the imposition of order in our thinking – which was Plato's contribution to Western civilization.

It would be unfair to claim that, because fascism in its more restrictive forms is an unacceptable method of government, fascism in thinking is equally unacceptable. Yet it is true that Western thinking is thoroughly fascist in its righteousness and certainty. The irony is that even when we think about democracy we think about it in a very rigid and defensive fascist way. We accept as sacrosanct certain aspects which are far from democratic. For example, in many countries people have very little say in the choice of a candidate to represent them and a final choice is restricted to a limited option of parties, with a rigid package of policies for each party. The purity of such systems is fiercely defended.

Given a choice between order and chaos, most people would choose order. Plato was impressed by the powerful order of the very fascist state of Sparta (whose citizens were allowed to kill their serfs once a year) which had just defeated Athens. The order put into thinking by Plato and the other members of the Gang of Three has been very attractive to subsequent thinkers. Yet today it may be time to move on. It may be necessary to make use of thinking methods which are more constructive and more creative. That is what I shall be exploring in this book.

4 THE DOUBTERS

It is important to understand the background that gave rise to the 'fascist' nature of the thinking of Plato and the Gang of Three. Largely, this thinking was a reaction to the current intellectual climate, which had been set by the sophists.

The sophists were a remarkably bright bunch of thinkers, but they have been very badly treated by history for a number of reasons. Some of the condemnation was deserved and some was not.

We do not, apparently, know too much about the sophists, because, in true fascist spirit, the followers of Plato suppressed the works of the sophists who had been roundly condemned by Plato.

The sophists were 'foreigners', having been born in Greek cities outside of Athens, and intellectual foreigners are never quite right. There was a suspicion and fear of these intellectuals because they were 'too clever by half'.

Then they charged fees for their instruction, which was not 'proper'. Why should teaching thinking or enlightenment be a paid profession other than in the law courts?

The main offence of the sophists was that they were too pragmatic. They needed to earn a living, and they realized that people would pay only for what was of practical value to them. So many of them concentrated on teaching rhetoric or the art of persuasion.

Greek culture was very oral. Interestingly, today with television and radio we are back in an oral culture, which is quite different from a written-word culture. So in Greece, at that time, being able to present a case and to persuade people was extremely important both in politics and in business. In essence, power came from persuasion.

Students were taught to argue on both sides of a case. Protagoras, a sophist, claimed that he could teach students how to make the 'weak' case overcome the 'strong' case. A high degree of persuasive skill could be taught. Wordplay was important. Obviously the boundary between honest wordplay in communication and dishonest wordplay does not exist, as politicians know only too well. So the sophists were rightly condemned for this aspect of 'trickery', even though, to this day, politics and law demand precisely the same 'persuasive' skills. That is the very nature of democracy. If people are not free to be fooled there is no democracy.

Some sophists taught only rhetoric. Others taught 'virtue' (skill in living a good life) as well. Some only taught 'virtue', in exactly the same sense as Socrates – but with a different approach.

The sophists were empiricists, sceptics, relativists and perceptualists in an amazingly modern way.

They believed that knowledge came only from experience. When asked about the existence of God, Protagoras replied that his faculties were too limited to take him to a conclusion on that matter and his life too short for the necessary search. Later he said that God existed for those who believed in God. The sophists believed that perception was the key. The only truth was perceptual truth. Protagoras said that the truth for any man was what he could be persuaded about.

If people are not free to be fooled there is no democracy.

The sophists preferred to deal in the constructed reality of 'beliefs' rather than the search for a fixed absolute truth. All perceptual beliefs were true, but not all were valid. So they were true for the person holding them but not necessarily valid for the outer world, everyone else and society. This was extreme subjectivism.

The relativism aspect held that truths held only in certain circumstances or games, which in a way antedated the Logical Positivists and Wittgenstein.

Of course, if truth was relative and perception was supreme then there was all the more reason for teaching the art of persuasion in order to change people's beliefs and perceptions.

There are many people today who would say that the sophists actually got it right and that the centuries of philosophical wordplay since then have been arabesques of futility taking us back precisely to the same point.

But could society work on the basis of doubt about everything; on the basis of subjective values; on the basis of truths which were only relative? Obviously it could not. There would be total chaos in which the skilled persuaders (taught by the sophists) would have the upper hand because they controlled perceptions and could fool people.

Society could not work in this way. So along came Socrates to show that truth was not subjective or relative but that there was a deep, fixed inner truth which was absolute and could be found by inquiry. Ironically, the new fascist democracy of Athens put Socrates to death because his method of inquiry seemed to undermine the 'old values' in precisely the way they were being undermined by the sophists. Yet he was seeking to do the exact opposite.

It was against this background that Plato emerged with his fascist views both on the State and on the state of the world. Things had to be absolute and things had to be ordered. He combined the belief of Heraclitus that everything was change with the opposite view of Parmenides that the inner essence never changed. He came up with his notion of absolute 'inner forms'. These were permanent, intrinsic truths 'to be discovered'.

There are many people today who would say that
the sophists actually got it right and that the centuries
of philosophical wordplay since then have been
arabesques of futility taking us back precisely to
the same point.

It is hardly surprising that the orderliness of Plato's ideas was taken up by most groups in society concerned with stable truths. Philosophers liked the framework because it gave them employment in the logical search for the elusive truths. The State, like any system of law, welcomed the notion of unchanging absolute principles. The Christian Church, strongly influenced by Paul, embraced the absolute truths and 'forms' and the rigidity of the system. So developed the convenience, practicality, comfort and success of the essentially fascist system of Western thinking.

Order was to be imposed by assuming that it was hidden as an absolute 'truth' to be discovered. This clever device of sincerely believing that an imposed order was really there all the time had a surprising pay-off in science, where the 'imposed order' (hypothesis) could be tested and changed with immense practical value. Elsewhere the fiction that we are looking for an 'inner truth' has seriously inhibited the design of better and more effective imposed orders. These do not have to take the form of fascist Utopias but may be enriched self-organizing systems (which we crudely approach with free-market philosophies and *laissez-faire*).

The important point to remember is that much of the hard-edged dogmatism of Western thinking methods came, via Plato, precisely as a reaction against the floppy subjectivity of the sophists.

5 THE SOCRATIC METHOD

If this book is concerned with the Socratic method, why have I been writing about Plato? Socrates (469 BCE to 399 BCE) was a historic figure who was ultimately condemned to death by the Athenian democracy on the grounds that he was 'corrupting the young'. He drank his cup of hemlock and passed into prominence in the history of philosophy and thought. This prominence, and dominance, is fascinating because Socrates never wrote anything at all. He just talked to people. What we know about Socrates was written by people who knew him. There was Xenophon, the practical military man. Through common friends there was Aristotle, the logician and philosopher – and also a member of the Gang of Three. Above all there was Plato.

Plato was not only a great thinker but also a brilliant writer. He conceived of the very clever device of expressing his thoughts in the form of dialogues between a character called Socrates and sundry others. Socrates as a character is by no means fiction, because there were many people alive who knew the real Socrates. The device both gave liveliness to what would otherwise have been boring philosophy and also protected Plato from direct attack. So we really know Socrates through Plato's writings in which Socrates is the dominating character.

Did Plato simply report, as from a tape recorder, what Socrates had said and thought? In some cases he undoubtedly did, or tried to the best of his ability and memory. Did Plato simply use Socrates as a mouthpiece for his own ideas? This is also obviously true in some cases, as in *The Republic*. Did Plato's own ideas form as a result of the influence of Socrates and so the ideas were anyway Socratic in origin and then re-expressed through the Socrates character? It seems most likely that Plato took over Socrates's ideas and methods, polished them up, added some of his own, and then gave them back to Socrates in the dialogues.

Plato had to stay within the bounds of reasonableness, otherwise the reports on Socrates from other sources would have contradicted Plato's version of Socrates. Nevertheless it is almost impossible to tease out what was really Socrates and what was really Plato. That is why it is essential to write about Plato.

What we call the 'Socratic method' is the Socratic method as expressed in Plato's writing, where the method is put into the mouth of Socrates by Plato but seems to relate well to the historic Socrates. Plato's excellence as a writer and thinker have also done more for Socrates than he could possibly have done for himself.

What truth are we seeking? How do we know when we have found it? Why do we believe there is a truth to be found?

What was the 'Socratic method'? Today we use this term in a rather broad sense to cover 'an endless search for the truth through asking questions'. But into this simple statement goes a real minestrone of factors. What truth are we seeking? How do we know when we have found it? Why do we believe there is a truth to be found? What sort of questions are we to ask? How do we judge and use the replies to the questions? How do we proceed from the replies to the truth? We find ourselves having to consider truth and untruth, judgement and refutation, definitions and boxes, induction, etc. Into all these matters enters the thinking not only of Socrates but also of Plato and of Aristotle as other members of the Gang of Three which gave us our traditional Western thinking system.

It is important to keep very clearly in mind that what I am considering in this book is not the quality or value of the ideas of Socrates/Plato but the thinking 'method' as such. There are times when the two are inseparable. For example, there has to be an assumption that there is a truth to be found – although the sophists, who were contemporaries of Plato, believed that there was no such thing and that truth was only what someone had been persuaded to believe. What we may regard as obvious today seems obvious only because we have been so indoctrinated with Plato's ideas. I shall only be considering 'ideas' in so far as they are essential to the 'method'.

When we have considered the Socratic method (the traditional Western thinking method), we may come to a number of possible conclusions:

1. That the method was very useful and valuable at the time, but today we can move on and do better.
2. That the method has a limited scope and is of value only in certain areas.
3. That the method is simply inadequate, since it leaves out many important aspects of thinking.
4. That the method is positively dangerous, because it locks us into a dangerous way of thinking about matters.
5. That the complacency and satisfaction with which we regard this method prevent us from developing more effective thinking methods.

There does not have to be a choice between these possibilities. In different ways and at different points all of them may be true. As the reader goes through this book, he or she will reach his or her own conclusions. It may also become obvious to readers what my own views happen to be.

At this point it is enough to say that I regard as dangerous and inadequate the complacency and contentment we often feel about this traditional thinking method. This complacency and contentment are not surprising, because, in a way, we are dealing more with a religious belief than with information-handling. The world view set out by the Gang of Three is a belief system which defends itself with the vigour of any religion that defends its tenets. It is not even possible to suggest that such tenets are wonderful but inadequate, because 'completeness' is a necessity in any belief system.

In the next section I shall consider the mechanics of the method.

6 HOW THE SOCRATIC METHOD WORKED

Socrates is credited with having brought philosophy down 'from the skies'. As a younger man he seems to have been interested in 'natural science', but he gave all that up to concentrate on much more practical matters such as morality, justice, love, politics, etc. Previous philosophers had been too much concerned with the stars, planets and other speculative amusements. Socrates firmly believed that this natural science had no practical value and was unknowable. This simple preference determined the path of Western philosophy for evermore.

Socrates was directly concerned with 'ethics'. He set out to establish standard and fixed definitions for such things as 'justice'. The background to this was that the contemporary sophists were extreme relativists and doubters. They claimed that things were only as you chose to see them. Thrasymachus in Plato's *The Republic* claims that morality is only a fancy word used to disguise the interest of the stronger group in society. How did Socrates set out to establish 'fixed' definitions which would remove the possibility of skilled persuaders leading people astray (as some sophists were training people to do)?

Imagine a small group of people who meet regularly to try to work out the grammar of a language which has always been spoken but never written. Various usages have evolved, and the group is trying to set out formal rules of grammar. Someone is asked to suggest a use. For example, how is 'to' used with an infinitive? The person asked suggests a general rule. Then the questioner produces examples which refute this rule. So a better rule is suggested. Then refuting examples are brought for that. And so on. This was roughly the method of Socrates.

> *Socrates:* Give me a definition of justice.
> *Reply:* Justice is giving back to a person what belongs to that person.
> *Socrates:* Just a moment. Suppose you borrow a knife from a friend and later that friend becomes mad and becomes violent. Should you then give the knife back to that friend?

This continual use of the counterexample was a characteristic of the Socratic method. Obviously this is very important with 'induction', because a single counterexample can destroy the definition.

It should at this point be said that most of the Socratic explorations ended in failure – that is, without any agreed definition as an outcome. This is hardly surprising. If we go back to the grammarians we would find that for any suggested 'rule' there would always be someone who could come up with a counterexample of a different usage. At some point a frustrated person would say: 'This is the best rule we can get and those counterexamples are simply mistaken usage.' But Socrates could not say that, for a number of reasons.

The Socratic method rests on the assumption that the knowledge is there, somewhere. This is by no means always the case.

In Plato's famous analogy of the cave, a person is chained up so that the person can see only the back wall of the cave.

At the mouth of the cave there is a fire. Another person comes into the cave carrying an object. The chained-up person cannot turn around but can see only the shadow of the newcomer-plus-object thrown on to the back wall of the cave. Similarly as we go through life we can see only shadows of the 'truth' or 'inner form'. So, unlike the grammarians, Socrates had to believe that all usages contained an element of the truth.

Socrates also made a virtue of ignorance. He had apparently been told by the oracle at Delphi that no man was wiser than Socrates. Eventually he concluded that this was because he alone knew of his ignorance. So he paraded his ignorance and was almost proud to have no conclusion to an exploration.

Then Socrates saw his role as a 'gadfly' to get people thinking about things and to weed out sloppy ideas. It was enough that his students should start to question and to think. The conclusion did not matter.

Aristotle considered the major contribution of Socrates to have been the method of induction leading to general definitions. In practice this meant listing a number of examples and then extracting a common feature. Ironically, this method is the basis of those sciences which are based on classification – like botany.

Socrates loved arguing from example. Sometimes the arguments were extremely dubious and fallacious and little more than skilled wordplay, but the general principle was to lead from example to conclusion.

Socrates: You would choose as steersman the most skilled
person on the ship, would you not? You would hardly
choose a steersman by drawing a lot, would you?
Reply: Of course not.
Socrates: You would choose your best athlete by testing
performance and not by lot. Is that not correct?

Reply: Assuredly so.

Socrates: So we should choose our politicians according to competence and not by lot?

Reply: Certainly.

Part of the Athenian political system was that the Council of Five Hundred was chosen by lot.

The argument seems powerful, but there is an underlying assumption that we are seeking 'competence' in politics as in steering a ship or in athletics. Suppose that we were seeking independence, neutrality, lack of bias, lack of power-group plays, lack of corruption. Then the choice by lot has much merit. It is also possible that people want not 'competent' government but government that they trust.

The above example, which is not an exact reproduction of the dialogue, also indicates a very curious phenomenon. The essence of the Socratic method is supposed to be the question. But Socrates himself very rarely used the Socratic method. His questions were rarely real questions. They were statements, to the end of which were tacked phrases like:

'Isn't that so?'

'Don't you agree?'

'Am I right about that?'

The so-called question was merely a request for affirmation or denial at the end of a statement.

Let us look at some of the replies extracted from Socratic dialogues as written up by Plato. The following replies are given by Simmias to statements/questions put by Socrates in the *Phaedo*:

'True.'

'Yes, endless examples.'

'Very true.'

'True.'

'Exactly so.'

'Yes, it may be derived so.'

'Very true.'

'We can say so with confidence.'

'To be sure.'

'Certainly.'

In *The Republic*, Adeimantus is replying to Socrates. Here are some replies interposed between the statements/questions of Socrates:

'Yes.'

'Yes.'

'What do you mean?'

'Yes.'

'True.'

'What objective?'

'They do say so.'

'Democracy does just that.'

'Certainly.'

Anyone reading through the Socratic dialogues has to be struck by the dominance of the statement/question, which could be typified by: 'We expect the sun to rise this morning as usual, ain't that so?'

It was enough that his students should start to question and to think. The conclusion did not matter.

Through a series of statements, each of which was relatively easy to agree with, Socrates led the student to a conclusion. Each step seems easy and to follow on from the previous step. The method is powerful, and is used every day by lawyers in court throughout the world. It is also highly dangerous and open to deceit and abuse. As with the example of the use of lots to choose politicians, it is easy to make a simple, unnoticed assumption and lead the argument to a false conclusion. How would the Socratic dialogues have proceeded if the student had used the following types of reply:

'Possibly.'

'Sometimes.'

'Under certain circumstances.'

'Not necessarily so.'

'Could be.'

Such replies admit possibility but deny the necessity which is required for this type of argument. But replying like this requires a great deal of creative skill, because the listener has to imagine circumstances where the statement is not always true.

If you have never seen and cannot imagine a black swan, how would you reply to the question, 'Swans are always white, are they not?'

You could say, 'As far as I know' or 'To the limits of my experience.'

But you could hardly say, 'Not necessarily' or 'Not always.'

I do not want to go into the merits or pitfalls of this type of reasoning. I merely want to indicate that the so-called Socratic questions were often not real questions at all.

Socrates saw himself as a 'midwife'. He did not feel that he had anything to teach. His role was to bring forth from the student knowledge that was already somewhere in the student's experience but confused, disorganized and unusable. Socrates, in a 'common search' with the student, was going to clarify beliefs, customs and principles and to extract fixed definitions. This was to be done through questions, challenges, examples, cross-examination and other tools of the 'endless search'.

The 'midwife' idiom is an attractive one and, not unnaturally, has appealed to educators throughout the ages. But it does rest on the assumption that the knowledge is there, somewhere. This is by no means always the case – even if it were in the field of ethics with which Socrates was concerned. In other areas it may be a very cumbersome way of teaching. There is, however, merit and attraction in what Socrates was really doing. This was to impart his own point of view and to do it in easy steps, with the student's acceptance at each step.

Socrates was trained as a sophist, and the sophists were much into rhetoric or the art of persuasion. Even though Plato, for obvious reasons, was vehemently opposed to the sophists, there are times when the arguments of Socrates in Plato's dialogues come very close to wordplay.

Socrates was concerned with the search for knowledge because to him knowledge was virtue. If knowledge was complete then no man could act in a harmful or improper manner. This has always been a circular argument (no harm in that), because whenever someone acts improperly we can always claim it is because of imperfect knowledge.

If a burglar knows that the chance of being caught is only about 1 in 20 then that knowledge could encourage burglary. But we could then say that if the burglar knew the effects on his psyche, or about his displeasing God, etc., then that 'true' knowledge would dissuade him. Similarly, 'true' knowledge might equip the burglar to make even more money in a legitimate way. The value of this belief of Socrates is not relevant here, except that it did activate his 'endless search for the truth'.

Socrates based a large number of his analogies on craftsmen who might be making pots, statues, boats, etc. He distinguished between the 'technical' expertise which was required and the 'virtue' with which the skill was used. So a technically adept craftsman might produce humdrum and boring pots. Beautiful pots required the addition of 'virtue'. So too in life, and it was the self-appointed mission of Socrates to develop this 'virtue' of living, through the birthing of knowledge helped by his midwife techniques.

Behind Socrates's seemingly innocent 'common search' for the truth through dialogue and questions there are many hidden habits and assumptions which I shall be examining in this book.

It should also be noted that I am concerned not solely with the pure or ideal Socratic method (which Socrates did not use) but with its practical evolution as what we use today as our version of that method. For instance we value highly criticism and argument, which are present as refutation in Socrates's dialogues but do not play nearly so dominant a part as in today's thinking.

7 THE SEARCH

Perhaps the most fundamental aspect of the Socratic method is the 'endless search for the truth'. To this can be attributed the volumes of philosophic introspection and the immense progress in science. This obsession with 'search' means that the journey may be more important than the destination, which is why Socrates was not at all bothered when his discourses reached no conclusion. In practice the endless search of the Socratic method has great merit because it means the sort of divine dissatisfaction which is the opposite of complacency and the essence of progress. It is fascinating that the one area to which we do not apply this dissatisfaction is the area of thinking and the Socratic method itself. We are complacent and defensive about this and do not seek better methods.

It is not too difficult to claim, but more difficult to prove, that the apparent advances in Western civilization compared to some others have been due to this 'search' component of intellectual effort. Other civilizations might rightly argue that for them value-preservation was more important than 'search for the truth'. Yet there is a Chinese proverb which says: 'Life is a search for the truth: there is no truth.'

In very broad terms, how is this search for the truth going to be carried out?

There are two general approaches:

1. Removal of 'untruth'.
2. Direct apprehension of the truth.

It will be necessary, later in this book, to consider what we mean by the 'truth' and what we think we are searching for. For the moment we will assume there is some sort of 'truth' worth finding.

The endless search of the Socratic method has great merit because it means the sort of divine dissatisfaction which is the opposite of complacency and the essence of progress.

The Hindus have a way of describing God entirely in negatives. That is to say they remove all 'untruths'. 'God cannot change.' 'God cannot be fooled.' The search for the truth by removing 'untruth' is a very dominant characteristic of Western thinking as well.

8 CRITICISM AND REMOVING 'UNTRUTH'

Imagine a prospector digging for gold in a dried-up riverbed. He removes the soil with his spade. Then he strikes a hard lump. Excitedly he washes the lump in his bucket. When the dirt has been washed away he is left with a shining nugget of gold. The process is simple. All he has to do is to remove the 'ungold' in order to reveal the gold.

So, too, in our thinking we are brought up to believe that all you need to do is to remove the 'untruth' by pointing out its untrue nature and then, eventually, you will be left with the shining truth.

You have a spotlessly clean bathroom. A child leaves a jammy handprint on the side of the bath. All you have to do is to remove the imperfection and you are left with the shining bath.

'You've got it wrong.'

'That is not what happened.'

'It simply ain't so.'

'It was not Gerald who asked.'

'The kiwi bird does not fly.'

'That does not follow.'

'Swans are not always white.'

'Raising the price does not always reduce sales.'

'Foreign aid is no way to develop a local economy.'

The word 'criticism' comes from the Greek '*kritikos*' which means 'able to judge'. Why then does the word 'criticism' tend to have a negative image and to suggest attack rather than objective judgement? Because criticism is almost always used in the negative sense. If you can point out the 'untruths' or false statements or false assumptions then you will be left with the truth – or at least on the way to the truth.

Where does this obsession of Western thinking with criticism and attack come from? It comes directly from Socrates. In his day Socrates got a terrible reputation for knocking down any idea or definition put forward but being unable, or unwilling, to offer any better suggestion. Apparently, Socrates thought it was enough to attack. At least this is how it seemed to his victims and some of his contemporaries.

It usually seemed that the essence of the Socratic method was to clear out errors, confusion and false assumptions rather than to bring forward better ideas. It was somewhat like the weeding process that may be necessary when a neglected garden is first tackled.

Socrates revelled in refutation. If anyone offered an idea – even a perfectly reasonable one – Socrates would scurry to put forward a counterexample, even if this involved very special circumstances (for example the matter of giving a knife back to a violent madman, mentioned earlier). His counterexamples made it very difficult to reach any conclusions at all. In a sense it may have been the honesty of Socrates which did not permit him to 'design' a possible answer but made him wait until the 'truth' revealed itself in spite of his efforts to counter it. The truth had to survive a sort of obstacle course put in place by Socrates's counterexamples.

The essence of the Socratic method was to clear out errors, confusion and false assumptions rather than to bring forward better ideas.

This challenge and 'shake-up' aspect of the Socratic approach may have been needed at the time, and it may even be needed today in some areas, but it has very largely got out of hand. There are far too many gardeners who strongly believe that 'weeding' is quite enough.

Western culture has always esteemed critical thinking far too highly. Amazingly, even today, there are people who regard critical thinking as the highest exercise of the human intellect. This is like saying that the last link in a chain is the most important one. I would, personally, place constructive thinking much higher, and there are some who would place creative thinking even higher.

Imagine six well-trained critical thinkers sitting around a table to discuss a new bridge. None of them can get going until someone actually puts a proposal or design on the table.

Why this obsession with the importance and sufficiency of critical thinking? There are a number of possible explanations.

1. The practical needs of education

Education is usually about youngsters sitting in classrooms and later in libraries. So education is usually about something which is put before the students. They are asked to 'react' to what is put before them. This reaction usually takes the form of critical comment. And the easiest form of the critical comment is the negative one.

2. Involvement and contribution

In a meeting or in a conversation any person who wants to contribute, to be involved or to be noticed has to say something. The easiest form of contribution is the negative:

'Yes, but ...'

'What about this danger?'

'In these circumstances it would not work.'

It is not difficult to focus on the 5 per cent that may not work instead of the 95 per cent that will work. From Socrates came the encouragement that even a far-fetched refutation was valid.

3. Emotional satisfaction

There is no doubt that criticism is very emotionally attractive and satisfying. Attacking an idea instantly makes you superior to that idea. The vandal who places a block of concrete on a rail line is temporarily superior to the designer of the high-speed train or the layer of the track. Criticism is a legitimate and useful cover for jealousy, as is so often the case in the academic world. Personal attacks and power plays can simply be given the cloak of genuine criticism.

4. Achievement

Criticism is one of the very few ways in which people who are not creative can achieve something and become influential. There are many drama critics who have become more significant than the playwrights themselves. The same applies to art critics.

5. It is very easy

It has to be said that criticism is very easy and is a relatively low form of intellectual effort. This comment does not cover the whole spectrum of criticism but only the bulk. If you set out to criticize it is not at all difficult to find something to criticize or to construct your own interpretation of what has been written or said or painted. By choosing a frame of judgement that is different from the architect's you can criticize the difference between the building and your selected frame. If the building is simple you can criticize it as being stark, boring and Bauhaus. If the building is elaborate you can criticize it as being frilly, vulgar, ostentatious and Victorian. If you cannot find anything to say you can always say it is derivative (meaning copying someone else) or repetitive (meaning copying its own designer). There is a whole repertoire of such remarks which are extremely easy to apply to anything and yet sound profound.

6. The world will go mad

There is a genuine, and not wholly unfounded, fear that if there were a let-up in criticism then the world would go mad. All sorts of fanciful ideas about extraterrestrials, spirit influences and economic cycles would emerge to take over. Just as Socrates felt that critical thinking was necessary to counter the pernicious influence of the deceiving sophists, so we still feel that intelligent people have the duty to guard society against both mad ideas and new ideas. The strategy is that new ideas should be criticized as fiercely as possible. If they survive then there may be some merit in them.

I am sure that there are many other reasons why critical attack is so appealing. It is less easy to see why we esteem it so very highly. Often it is indeed necessary to point out why something does not fit the facts, our experience or our values. Often it is necessary to point out that something does not follow or does not necessarily follow. These are highly useful operations, and we may feel that if we get our 'truth mechanisms' right then all else will be right too. It may be that criticism carries relatively little risk as compared with any sort of constructive or creative effort. So criticism is rarely going to be seen as 'wrong'.

There are far too many gardeners who strongly believe that 'weeding' is quite enough. Western culture has always esteemed critical thinking far too highly. Amazingly, even today, there are people who regard critical thinking as the highest exercise of the human intellect.

Nevertheless it does seem an absurd assumption that removing faults and errors is sufficient intellectual behaviour for society.

A car driver who makes no errors is not necessarily a good driver. He or she might keep the car in the garage all the time and so avoid any possible error.

A person who is tied up tightly with a rope cannot possibly play the violin. If we remove the rope, does that person automatically become a violinist?

Why do we assume that removing bad things is enough to create good things? It may be because somewhere in our mind there is that metaphor of the prospector digging for gold or the jammy handprint on the bath. Remove what is incorrect and you will be left with the truth. This was very much part of the Socratic method.

So should we conclude that refutation, negative criticism and attack are a bad thinking habit? Not at all. I have used that very method to criticize the method itself. Criticism is a valuable and essential part of thinking, just as the front left wheel is a rather necessary part of the car.

Nevertheless, we need to realize that critical thinking is totally inadequate by itself. We need to reduce our obsession with critical thinking. We need to question the high esteem in which we hold critical thinking. We need to be very critical of critical thinking, realizing that it is often a cheap and easy exercise. We need to understand that the easy use of critical thinking makes very difficult the emergence of new ideas. This is particularly so when a new idea needs to be judged within a new paradigm not within the old paradigm which, by definition, it does not fit.

On a practical note, we should observe that cheap and easy criticism in the media succeeds only in devaluing success, achievement, politics and people to the point where society as a whole becomes demoralized.

How would the 'parallel-thinking' method handle this matter? The emphasis would be on 'caution'. It would be a matter of pointing out possibilities:

'We need to be careful about that.'

'We need to be cautious under these circumstances.'

'That may work out differently.'

'Here is another possibility.'

Parallel thinking does not need the harsh sharp-edged judgements that are required by the 'truth merchants' in the Socratic system. The true/false dichotomy is softened by 'possibility', overlap and fuzzy edges. Alternative views can lie alongside each other – in parallel.

9 ADVERSARIES, ARGUMENT AND DEBATE

It was Clausewitz, the Prussian military philosopher, who observed that, 'War is merely the continuation of politics by other means.' We could say of our traditional habit of argument that it is 'the continuation of war by other means'.

The argument method of thinking has been the curse of Western civilization, and yet it is a method we treasure and esteem highly. The method arises directly from the belief that if you remove the 'untruth' or 'bad things' then the truth will lie revealed. Therefore it is enough to attack. It is enough to prove the other fellow wrong, since that other fellow is trying to do the same to you. Through this method of mutual attack the truth is somehow going to be laid bare.

We use the adversarial argument method in parliaments and legislative assemblies of any sort. The court procedure in many countries (but not all) is based on the adversarial system. There is argument in business decision-making and in negotiation. There is argument in family discussions. Not only does this happen but we encourage it to happen. Schools are proud of their debating teams. We regard as heroes those who debate powerfully or subtly. Surely this wonderful system is the very essence of the Western thinking tradition?

There may be a place for the pantomime and theatre of spirited political debate, but is that really the best way to be constructive? In most countries many politicians are lawyers. There are at least two reasons for this. Firstly, lawyers are trained to argue and therefore fit easily into the system and in so doing reinforce the argument mode. Secondly, unlike doctors or business executives, a lawyer can slip into politics and then out again to continue practising law. In most professions or occupations that is not possible. So it is little wonder that 'lawyer-type' argument has remained the style of visible government – what goes on invisibly is somewhat more cooperative.

Argument is the very essence of dialectic. There must be two sides to every question. From the clash between thesis and antithesis comes the synthesis – or does it?

On a major television programme in Australia an argument was deliberately set up between myself and the leading American proponent of critical thinking. This was because television has come to believe that interest can be generated only by clash or argument. The time could have been better spent in a constructive exploration of the important subject of teaching thinking in schools. Yet the audience gave that programme the highest rating it had ever had (or so I was told). Wrestling, boxing and argument may be good spectator sports.

It could be pointed out that I have focused on the more extreme forms of adversarial argument and that there are many gentler discussions in which a genuine attempt is made to explore the subject. It could be said that the 'proper' use of argument is not in the adversarial mode, therefore these 'fierce' arguments are not really true arguments. I would maintain that if a method is so easily abused and so rarely used 'properly' then that method is faulty and there is little point in saying that it ought to be used 'properly'. Hope is not always sufficiently practical.

Once the battle is joined, ego and winning become much more important than exploring the subject.

From where did this habit of argument come? Socrates had the reputation of being a pugnacious sort of fellow who was always out to challenge or refute what others said. In real life he may indeed have been argumentative, but as written up by Plato in the dialogues Socrates comes across as gentle and considerate. Socrates insists on the 'common search' in which both he and the students together tease out the true definition of whatever is being explored. It may be that Plato was being nice to Socrates. It is also true that Socrates was gentle with his students but more pugnacious with his peers. It may be that the argument system required the unusual personality of Socrates to give it the appearance of a genuine exploration, but that without that personality, and humility, it becomes an adversarial fight. All in all, I do not think we can blame Socrates for the argument system as such.

This time we have to blame the sophists, who did regard argument as a veritable 'verbal battle' from which one side would emerge as a victor while the other side would be annihilated. There had to be a win/lose outcome, otherwise how could the sophists show that their training was worth the money paid for it? The sophists would train their students to argue with equal success on both sides of the issue. As with lawyers today, argument and case-making was all that mattered.

Over the centuries the argument habit was picked up, polished and used by the great thinkers of the Christian Church for their battles with heretics. It might even be argued that the interest that people such as Thomas Aquinas showed in Aristotelian logic arose from its value as an argument device.

Like criticism, argument is emotionally attractive. It puts into a more civilized framework the joy of fighting and the potential joy of destroying the other party. Once this innate

Argument

attractiveness had been legitimized as the proper way to think about things it is no surprise that argument became so pervasive in Western culture. Other cultures do have discussions and disagreements and emotions, but without division into two warring parties.

The best thing to be said in favour of the adversarial system is that it motivates exploration of a subject. Because both parties are motivated by the win/lose nature of debate there is supposed to be thorough examination of the subject. In addition the adversaries have to watch carefully what they are saying, for fear of being challenged. There is the underlying assumption that one point of view can never explore a subject but is only a sales pitch. Two opposing points of view will therefore cover the subject fully. This is another of our quaint beliefs.

Argument freezes people into positions, and then they are imprisoned by those positions.

The trouble with adversarial argument is that as the motivation to 'win' rises so the exploration of the subject declines. Lawyers in court are interested in making a case and winning the case, not in exploring the subject. If one lawyer happens to think of a point which would benefit the other side, that point is never going to be brought out. Participants in school debates are more interested in making debating-points than in exploring the subject. Showing that the other party is wrong or stupid is not a great contribution to the exploration of the subject. Once the battle is joined, ego and winning become much more important than exploring the subject. The involvement of the ego in the argument method as a way of getting motivation quickly becomes self-defeating.

Like many thinkers, Socrates (or Plato) had an almost mystical belief in dichotomies, polarities and opposites. At one point Socrates argues for the immortality of the soul on the basis that, just as sleep follows waking and waking follows sleep, so death follows life and life must follow death. Similarly there is a true/false dichotomy, so if one side is proved to be false in an argument then it must seem that the other side is true. In practice, as most people know, both sides are usually wrong, because of their limited perspective.

Argument freezes people into positions, and then they are imprisoned by those positions. Argument encourages cleverness at the expense of wisdom. It is very difficult to imagine a clever person arguing:

'You are right under those circumstances.'

'That may well happen some of the time.'

'That fits with the definition you hold.'

'If you choose those values you are right.'

Wisdom is more concerned with genuine exploration and has no need for the absolutes of hard-edged righteousness.

If argument is so appalling a system – and I believe it is appalling – what can we do about it?

In the matter of criticism, I suggested that it has a high value but that we should not be obsessed by it and should not feel that removing the bad is sufficient. In the matter of argument, I feel we should simply drop the method entirely, because it is not only a poor way of exploring a subject but also locks us into dangerous and unproductive polarities.

Many developed countries ban cock-fights and dog-fights. I suggest we do the same with adversarial argument.

So what are we going to put in the place of adversarial argument? There have always been court systems in some countries that use the exploratory 'inquisitorial' method rather than the adversarial.

As a general substitute for the head-on clash of adversarial argument I would suggest that we adopt the method of 'parallel' thinking, which I shall describe in the next section.

10 PARALLEL THINKING

'*Parallel* thinking' is a broad term that covers the alternative thinking method that I am proposing as a replacement for the traditional Socratic method. In this section I shall be considering one specific aspect of parallel thinking. It is an aspect which makes clear the nature of parallel thinking and why and how it is different from the Socratic method. Nevertheless, it should be kept in mind that parallel thinking covers much more than the aspect covered in this section. Other aspects of parallel thinking will be met in later sections of the book.

Parallel thinking simply means laying down ideas alongside each other. There is no clash, no dispute, no initial true/false judgement. There is instead a genuine exploration of the subject from which conclusions and decisions may then be derived through a 'design' process.

It is not much use condemning the traditional adversarial argument method without offering something practical in its place. That is the prerogative of those who feel it is enough to criticize. Moreover, what is offered in place of traditional adversarial argument must be attractive and easy to use.

The method described here has been very rapidly taken up and is now in use with a wide variety of thinkers, ranging from eight-year-olds at Norfolk Academy (a prestigious school in Virginia) to senior executives in such major corporations as DuPont, IBM, Prudential, etc. I am told that the leading black newspaper in

South Africa, the *Sowetan*, uses the method at its editorial board meetings. I have also been told that the Mormon Church uses it at some of its senior meetings. The method is used by schoolchildren in Florida (and many other places); by executives and public servants in Singapore; by thinkers in Italy, Argentina and many other places. At one meeting in Shanghai the head of the government's policy unit was so enthusiastic about the method that he promised to take it back to Beijing to shorten meetings that sometimes lasted 19 hours. In Japan, at the time, the most highly valued corporation in the world (NTT) was an early user of the method because the chief executive immediately saw its value.

So the method is not a strange new idea that has just been dreamed up. It is in use with a wide variety of ages, backgrounds, cultures, etc. In fact, from a cultural point of view it already has a much wider spread than the Western argument mode, which is unacceptable in many cultures.

The method is the 'Six Hats' method.

There are six metaphorical hats, each of a different colour. The thinker uses one hat at a time and follows, exclusively, the mode of thinking indicated by the hat.

Parallel thinking simply means laying down ideas alongside each other. There is no clash, no dispute, no initial true/false judgement. There is instead a genuine exploration of the subject.

At first the idea of coloured hats may seem silly and childish, but there is an absolute perceptual need for some 'concrete' framework to make the method easy to use and easy to remember. Exhortation without the symbolism is weak and useless.

The white hat indicates information. You can think of white paper. White is neutral. When the 'white hat' is in use, everyone at the meeting focuses, in parallel, on laying out the information. What information is available? What information is needed? What information is missing? How are we going to get the information we need? The quality of information can range from hard, checkable facts to rumour or opinion. The quality should be indicated. When there are disagreements, the different versions are simply laid down alongside each other. If the matter is vital, it can be checked out later.

'The evening plane to London leaves at 19.00.'

'The evening plane to London leaves at 20.00.'

'There is no dispute, challenge or argument at the time.'

The red hat indicates feelings, emotions, intuition and hunches. You can think of red as fire and warmth and feelings. The red hat legitimizes the expression of feelings and intuition. In a normal discussion you are not expected to bring in feelings unless they can be justified. Under the red hat the justification or explanation of feelings or intuition is not permitted. The feelings or intuition are expressed as they exist:

'I feel this investment is not going to work.'

'I feel she is the right person for the job.'

'My intuition tells me that will not be accepted.'

The red hat indicates feelings at the moment. From the beginning of a meeting to the end of a meeting, feelings can change. Intuition and feelings are not always right. Intuition can be based on a complex experience of the field, and it may not be possible to itemize the factors behind the intuition. Under the red hat, intuition has the right to exist. Feelings also have the right to exist visibly. They exist invisibly, so why should they not be made visible? In normal argument, feelings are expressed through attack or enthusiasm. With the hat system, feelings are expressed directly – without guilt or apology.

The black hat is the most widely used hat, and possibly the most valuable. I write this because many people wrongly assume that the black hat is somehow a bad hat. It is certainly nothing of the sort. For black, think of a judge's robes, which are usually black. The black hat is for caution, for risk assessment and for criticism. This is an essential part of thinking if we are not to make mistakes and do things which are dangerous to ourselves or damaging to others. We use the black hat to see whether something fits our information, our experience, our objectives, our policy, our values, our ethics, etc.

The trouble is that the black hat can be overused by those who believe that it is enough to criticize. So it is important to distinguish between the high value of the black hat when used appropriately and the danger of excessive use. This is exactly the same point that I made about the use of criticism. Food is necessary, but too much food is harmful. Wine is excellent, but too much wine is harmful.

The yellow hat indicates the 'logical positive'. Yellow may suggest sunshine and optimism. With the yellow hat everyone looks, in parallel, for benefits and values. Under the yellow hat there is an effort to see how something can be done. Both the yellow and the black hat require logical support. You do have to spell out the reasons behind your statements. The yellow hat is much harder than the black hat, because it is natural to point out difficulties and dangers but much less natural to search for values.

The green hat is for creative effort. Think of green and vegetation and growing: branches, shoots, etc. The green hat makes time and space for deliberate creative effort. Under the green hat there is a search for alternatives and for new ideas. Under the green hat go provocation, 'movement' and the specific processes of lateral thinking. Above all, the green hat is concerned with 'possibility'.

'Possibility' may be the most important word in thinking. It is the power of 'possibility' that is responsible for Western technical progress – not the argument system. Possibility covers the hypothesis device in science. Possibility provides frameworks for perception and for arranging ideas and information. Possibility allows speculation. Possibility permits vision. I shall be dealing further with many of these points later.

Finally there is the blue hat. Think blue sky and overview. The blue hat is the hat for thinking about thinking and managing the thinking process. Just as the conductor seeks to get the best out of the orchestra, so the blue hat seeks to orchestrate the thinking process. The blue hat would typically be used by the chairperson or facilitator at a meeting, but anyone can make suggestions about procedure under the blue hat.

It is all very simple. But it works very well. Why? Partly because it is so simple. There are many other reasons as well.

1. Thinking in parallel

At no point is there any attempt to disagree, to challenge or to dispute a point. Statements and ideas are put down in parallel, alongside each other. Everyone is focused in the same 'direction' and is thinking cooperatively, in parallel.

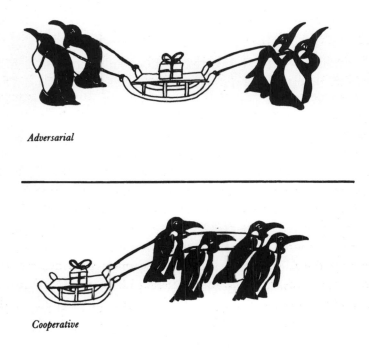

Adversarial

Cooperative

2. No politics and power play

Power plays and personal attacks are simply not possible in the system. People who have exerted their authority through attack now have to generate ideas.

3. Time and space for creativity

Instead of someone trying to squeeze in an idea, there is now time and space allotted to deliberate creative effort. This means that everyone is expected to make some sort of creative effort.

4. Caution in its place

It is no longer possible to jump on an idea as soon as it is presented. The idea can be subjected to full critical scrutiny, but only at the right time. It is no longer a strategy to sit there and be negative about everything.

5. Expression of feeling

The red hat permits the direct expression of intuition and feeling in a way that is simply not possible in traditional thinking. The red hat also allows someone to ascertain feelings at any point.

6. Searching for value

Usually when an idea is proposed the dangers come to mind more easily and ahead of the values. So the idea can get dismissed. The yellow hat provides a means for directing a deliberate search for values and benefits in a proposal.

7. Thinking about thinking

The blue hat provides a mechanism for thinking about thinking and for structuring the thinking process instead of just drifting from point to point.

8. Removal of the ego

A major problem with traditional thinking is the intrusion of the ego. Few people are willing to find good points in an idea they oppose. Few people who are enthusiastic about an idea want to look for the dangers in the idea. The Six Hats method challenges the ego to give a good performance under the designated hat. So a person who dislikes the idea is still expected to put in a good yellow-hat performance and to find the values in the idea.

9. Use of full intellectual power

In the usual divisions of the argument structure, only half those present (or some other ratio) are actually looking for the weak points in the idea – or the benefits. With the Six Hats method all the intellectual 'horsepower' present is used in each direction.

10. One thing at a time

Normally, in thinking, we try to do everything at once. We seek to be creative, critical, information-oriented all at the same time. The Six Hats method allows us to focus on doing one thing at a time and doing it properly, with full attention. This is not unlike full-colour printing, where the basic colour separations are printed one by one on top of each other.

11. Shortened meeting times

Because of the parallel focus and parallel thinking, a lot of the normal time-wasting interchanges are eliminated. One IBM laboratory found that the method reduced meeting times by 75 per cent. In practice it is amazing how much thinking can take place in as short a time as two minutes if there is a parallel effort rather than an argument effort.

12. Opportunity to switch

Surprisingly, many habitual black-hat thinkers welcome the method because it allows them to switch from the black hat to, for example, the green hat. They no longer have to be critical all the time. They can also show how they can be creative – and often they are creative once the effort is made.

13. Organizing thinking

The method provides a means for talking about thinking and for organizing thinking. Instead of a general free-for-all, there is the possibility of designing the optimal sequence, which will differ from subject to subject.

14. Freedom

People welcome the freedom from having to defend or attack an idea at every moment. They are much more free to explore the subject.

There is some suggestion that the biochemical balances in the brain may be different when we are thinking cautiously from when we are thinking positively and from when we are thinking creatively. If this turns out to be so then there is an absolute need to use something like the Six Hats method, because the brain cannot have the optimal setting for each of the different modes of thinking at the same time. It is like playing golf: you need the different golf clubs. There is no one super-club which would allow you to putt and drive with the same club.

Emotions change our thinking by setting different sensitivities in the brain. If you are angry you will look at things in a different way from when you are pleased. In a way, the hats provide a sort of 'external emotion' which sensitizes our minds to look at things in a range of different ways – instead of from just one perspective.

The hats provide a very practical means for shifting from the right/wrong basis of argument to exploration. The exploration is systematic and thorough.

'Possibility' may be the most important word in thinking. It is the power of 'possibility' that is responsible for Western technical progress – not the argument system.

It is very important to note that the hats do not indicate types or categories of people. It is true that some people may habitually seem to wear the black hat. It is true that some people prefer the green hat. It is true that some people may feel they function better under the white hat. All that does not matter at all. The hats are definitely not classifications of people. The idea of a hat is that it is easily put on and easily taken off. So the hats indicate temporary behaviour patterns. Everyone needs to try to use the hat indicated at that moment. At first this may seem awkward and contrary to a normal thinking habit, but, in time, people get better and better at using all the hats.

In the Western world we often seek to change behaviour by changing people first. So if someone is aggressive we may seek to make that person less aggressive. The Confucian approach was to focus directly on the desired behaviour. The Six Hats method does the same. If a person is aggressive then let that person be aggressive, but when the yellow hat is in use then the aggression is used to discover value. This is one of the aspects of the method which has made it so acceptable.

The Six Hats framework should be treated as a sort of 'game' (set of rules). In this way it becomes 'self-monitoring'. Each person wants to follow the 'rules' of the game and feels foolish if he or she is seen to be doing the wrong thing at any time.

The hats can be used singly as a means for aligning the thinking of the group in one direction for a short time. For example, at some point there may be a need to look for further alternatives – 'Let's have some green-hat thinking here.' At another time there may be a need to ask for some black-hat thinking, to examine the risks in a proposed course of action.

The hats can also be used systematically in a chosen sequence so that one hat follows the other. The sequence will vary from subject to subject and according to who is present at the meeting. There are certain guidelines regarding the setting-up of sequences but no fixed 'ideal sequence'.

It has been my intention here simply to indicate, in broad terms, how the Six Hats method of parallel thinking works. Those who are interested in reading further about the method or its application should consult the footnote.[*]

The main point about the method is that it is in wide use and works well. It is not just a theory but a practical system in daily use. What it does is provide a concrete alternative to the traditional adversarial argument system and to formless point-to-point discussion which wanders aimlessly all over the place.

The Six Hats method uses parallel thinking in three ways:

1. Under a designated hat, everyone in the group is thinking in parallel in the same direction. The thinkers are looking at the subject, not at each other's thinking about the subject.
2. Different opinions, even if contradictory, are laid alongside each other and are to be considered later, if necessary.

---

[*] See my book *Six Thinking Hats* (London: Penguin, 2000). For training courses, please visit: www.edwdebono.com.

3. The hats themselves provide parallel directions for looking at the subject. For example the yellow hat and the black hat are parallel efforts to assess the difficulties and to assess the benefits. They are not opposed to each other.

Surprisingly often the use of the hats leads directly to an outcome from the meeting. At other times there is a need to apply a 'design' process to produce an outcome from the exploration or a 'decision' process to obtain a decision. The thorough exploration of the parallel-thinking process makes these further steps very much easier.

So there is a practical alternative to adversarial argument. There may be times when one or other mode is more appropriate, but we no longer have to use traditional argument because there is 'no other way'. There *is* another way now – and it works very well.

11 PROBLEM-SOLVING

Most of the major problems in the world today persist precisely because we have such an excellent method of problem-solving. This statement is not intended to be sarcastic. We do have an excellent method of problem-solving. It is so good, however, that we have come to believe that it will solve all problems. So we have not bothered to develop any other method. The good is often the enemy of the best. If something is very good then we stop there and cloak ourselves in complacency.

What is this excellent, traditional, method of problem-solving? It is yet another example of the basic belief that if you 'remove the bad things' you will be left with the good things.

So the general method is that you analyse the problem, identify the cause and then proceed to remove the cause. The cause of the problem is removed so the problem is solved. It works.

If you have a sore throat you identify the bacteria as a streptococcus. You take penicillin to kill the streptococcus. You have removed the cause and you get better.

You feel a sharp pain when you sit down on a chair. You examine the cushion and find a pin. You remove the pin and the problem is solved.

You analyse the problem of inflation and find that it is caused by excess money supply and too high a velocity of circulation of money. So you remove the cause by making money more expensive with high interest rates. You have cured inflation.

You may, of course, also have caused a recession by driving out of business many small operations that cannot survive the high interest rates, but that does not matter.

The general method is simple and it works well, when it works. But there are some problems where you cannot find the cause. There are other problems where there are so many causes that you cannot remove all of them. Then there are problems where you can find the cause but you cannot remove it. Perhaps you cannot remove the cause because it is human nature, and you cannot easily remove that.

What do we do in such cases? We just try harder. We try harder with yet more analysis. We try harder to remove the cause. A classic example is the drug problem, where there are many causes that cannot be removed. So we try harder to remove the cause.

While acknowledging the excellence of the general method of solving a problem by identifying and removing the cause, we also need to do something about those instances where the method simply does not work. Are these insoluble problems? Possibly, but we ought at least to try some other methods.

Given our technical competence, how much further ahead would we have been with a more constructive thinking style?

An alternative method is to leave the cause in place and to 'design' a way forward. We do not like doing this. There are two reasons for this dislike. The first is a rather 'purist' reason. We believe that if the cause is still in place then our solution is just papering over the cracks and is only cosmetic. It is as if the cause is a sort of 'untruth' which cannot be tolerated. The second reason is that designing the way forward requires new concepts and creativity. This is difficult, and we do not like creativity because we prefer to feel that analysis is sufficient.

The whole thrust of education is towards analysis. Everything should yield to analysis in our traditional methods of thinking. Very little emphasis is given to creativity.

Can we design a system in which inflation cannot happen? I believe we can.

Can we find different approaches to the drug problem? Possibly.

Is there a better approach to the sort of civil war that has devastated Iraq? There may be.

I am not going to offer wonderful new ideas, because an idea is only a product. What I am suggesting is that we invest more time and effort in the approach to problem-solving by designing the way forward. For example, I would like to see the United Nations set up a Creative Resource which could provide a creative framework, and creative training, in order to help UN agencies and member countries develop some skill at this approach to problem-solving. I would like to see schools and universities devote some part of education to this matter. It is absurd to go on believing that analysis is sufficient.

We apply the general idiom of 'remove the bad' to many situations. Our intellectuals are trained to be 'against things'. It is enough to be against pollution. It is enough to be against racial discrimination. In some cases it is indeed enough. Values do change. People do feel guilty about smoking. Bad things do get curbed or even removed. The idiom does have its place.

Being against things is not enough. We also need to develop the habits of constructive thinking.

This idiom was enough to get rid of the Shah of Iran, General Somoza in Nicaragua, President Marcos in the Philippines, the dictatorship in Somalia, apartheid in South Africa and the communist regime in the USSR. Once these bad things were removed then it was assumed everything would be wonderful. Like removing the jammy handprint on the bath and being left with the pristine cleanness there was before.

Most revolutions are against something. That gives a target, focus, energy and a sense of mission. But when the 'bad things' are gone, what happens next? Only too often there is confusion or a state of affairs that seems, at least temporarily, to be worse than before. Is this an argument for keeping bad things in place? Should Colonel Gaddafi have stayed in Libya?

My point is that being against things is not enough. We also need to develop the habits of constructive thinking. But we do not. Educated people are well trained to be against things but poorly trained to be constructive. Being constructive is for artists or those materialistic people who want to make money in business. This is all part of the traditional thinking system that really does believe that analysis and argument are enough. Given our technical competence, how much further ahead would we have been with a more constructive thinking style?

We naïvely believe that the good things (like truth) are already there, obscured by bad things or hidden from sight. Search is enough. Being constructive is irrelevant. All that comes from the traditional thinking system set up by the Gang of Three. Should we not move on?

12 THE EVOLUTION OF IDEAS

We are very wary of 'designed' ideas. Utopians are looked upon with great suspicion. This is hardly surprising when one looks at the horrific Utopian state that the great Plato designed in his *The Republic*. We are much more comfortable with evolution. Small changes here and there and different pressures over time are assumed to be enough to keep existing ideas in tune with a changing world and to bring about new ideas as they become needed.

Then there is another source of new ideas. This is the mysterious energy of a mysterious group of people who will forever be putting forward new ideas because their motivation inclines them that way. It is enough for the 'guardians' to knock back these ideas and to criticize them, for the bad ones to be suppressed and the tolerable ones to be moulded into usefulness.

Both these sources of ideas suggest that there is no need to develop any active skill in constructing, designing or creating ideas. It is enough to exercise restraint and judgement. This is a safe approach, and is unlikely to lead to any disasters like the poll tax idea that was the undoing of Mrs Thatcher as prime minister. No one can be blamed for evolution and slow change and ideas that survive the harshest criticism.

The underlying assumption, however, is that the world is not changing very much and that slow evolution will take care of slow changes. But if nothing much is done then the gap between existing ideas and the fast-changing world can get enormous.

It is rather like being afraid to make a decision for fear of getting it wrong and being criticized. It seems safer not to make a decision. But not making a decision is itself a decision, and sometimes a very dangerous one.

On the whole, governments prefer 'crisis management'. Do nothing until the crisis is visible to everyone. Then whatever you do appears to have been forced by circumstances beyond your control. That is how Britain came to leave the ERM (the Exchange Rate Mechanism of the European Monetary System). There is much practical sense in this strategy, but few governments would acknowledge that such a strategy was in place.

Yet with ideas we openly use that strategy. Do nothing until a crisis forces action. At that point you will get support for almost any action that is taken to alleviate the crisis.

This then adds a third mode of change, but one which does require some creativity – which usually has to be exercised in a hurry, and in a 'problem-solving' mode rather than a 'design' mode. In other words, the ideas produced to alleviate the crisis have to have an immediate palliative action, often at the expense of their long-term suitability.

We usually believe that if you are right at one point then all you have to do is to move forward. This is not so. You may need to move back to change something which was perfectly right at the time.

I suspect that in most countries most people would feel that:

- it is possible to have a better education system;
- it is possible to have a better healthcare system;
- it is possible to have a faster judicial system;
- it is possible to have a fairer tax system;
- it is possible to have more democratic government;
- it is possible to do more about pollution.

Sometimes this would simply mean that the citizen wanted more money spent on a particular sector in order to use the existing ideas better. In fewer cases there might be a desire for a real change in the system. In fact both types of wish demand new ideas. Most governments are under tight budgetary control and so it is usually not possible just to put more money into one area. Instead of money there may need to be better ideas, in order to get more value out of the existing budget.

At the time of writing both Malaysia and Singapore use the concept of the Central Provident Fund (CPF). In Singapore both employer and employee contribute 20 per cent of wages to this fund. The accumulated lump sum is then payable on retirement. Meanwhile the worker can borrow against this money for certain specified purposes such as housing, healthcare, education and investment. The idea seems sensible because it provides a retirement lump sum and also provides the government with a huge amount of capital. At the same time it introduces 'targeted' spending so that some part of a person's earnings can only be spent in specified ways.

I am told that the idea originated in colonial days when labour was imported from India. Both the worker and the employer had to pay some money into a fund that was set aside to pay for the return passage of the worker to India.

In many countries it would be politically impossible to introduce the CPF concept even if the merits were appreciated. Yet such a concept is unlikely to arise from evolution.

The weakness of evolution is that once a direction has been set we proceed in that direction until it proves utterly disastrous. This principle can be illustrated in a simple way involving a sequence of pieces which are presented one or two at a time. At each moment the receiver has to make the 'best use' of what is available. In other words, at each moment the best logical decision must be made. The sequence is shown in Figure 3 overleaf. The first two pieces are best arranged as a rectangle and the ratio of the sides can be declared if required. The next piece is simply added on to give a longer rectangle. This is a sensible, logical decision. Then the next two pieces arrive and we fit them in as best we can. The result is far from satisfactory. We have, however, been committed in that direction.

Had we been allowed to go back and change an arrangement which had been 'the best at the time', we might then have produced a square and the final arrangement would have been a satisfactory larger square – as shown.

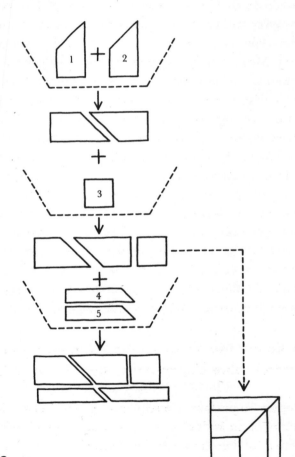

Figure 3

This very simple demonstration illustrates a fundamental principle. In any system in which information comes in over time and there is a need to make the best use of it at every moment, there is an absolute need to be able to go back and rearrange the components in order to make the best use of the available information. This is one of the logical reasons why we need 'creativity'.

Nor is it any use some super-smart person claiming that at the second stage he or she would have formed the square. This would not have been any more useful, because there was no knowledge of what was going to come next. For example, if the next piece had been the small one shown then the square would have needed reorganizing.

The inescapable fact is that evolution without the possibility of going back and changing ideas which were 'the very best at the time' is bound to be extremely inefficient.

Unfortunately it is not as easy simply to go back to rearrange the pieces as suggested in the figure. In real life the pieces do not remain separable but have come together as a concept, a method, an institution or a principle. The component pieces are no longer visible or rearrangeable.

The consequences of this simple principle are rather important. We usually believe that if you are right at one point then all you have to do is to move forward. This is not so. You may need to move back to change something which was perfectly right at the time. Similarly our emphasis on preserving tradition may be misplaced where it is more than just cosmetic.

We do not like pluralism, because Socrates and company have convinced us there is only one 'truth'.

Another important consequence is the realization that no amount of 'tinkering' with an existing idea will suddenly change it into a fundamentally different idea. The new idea may require a basic rearrangement of the components.

It is also possible to claim that no idea can ever make the best use of its components, since these have arrived in a particular sequence over time and that sequence of arrival plays too large a part in the final arrangement. Theoretically all the components would have needed to be present simultaneously.

But what are the practical outcomes from these realizations and considerations?

One outcome is the understanding that radical changes are sometimes essential. What was wonderful and the best in its time may need to be radically changed. But how do you change from something which is adequate, or which people have come to accept as adequate, to something that is unknown and risky? If the existing idea is the best then we should keep it. If the new idea is better then we must change. We are tied here to the either/or and true/false dichotomies that underly our thinking.

So what is the 'parallel' approach? The answer is very literal. You introduce the new idea 'in parallel' or alongside the old idea. You allow both to coexist. You might even give people the option of choosing. If the new idea is valuable, over time it will then gain force.

Yet this simple strategy is almost impossible in practice. Why? Because we have been taught to want the 'one truth'. Both ideas or methods cannot be 'right'. One must be right and the other must be wrong.

This thinking is so deeply inbred in us that we regard it as inevitable and natural. Yet it is part of the 'belief system' arising from the sort of thinking determined by the Gang of Three.

I freely acknowledge that there may at times be practical difficulties in allowing different ideas/methods to coexist. That, however, is not the real problem, because practical difficulties can sometimes be overcome. The difficulties are intellectual. We do not like pluralism, because Socrates and company have convinced us there is only one 'truth'.

13 THE SEARCH FOR THE TRUTH

In a previous section I mentioned that there seemed to be two fundamental approaches to the search for the truth. The first was the removal of 'untruth'. It was enough to remove untruth and all manner of 'bad things' and then the true and the good would lie revealed. I sought to examine some of the consequences of that belief: excessive love of criticism; the adversarial argument system; and problem-solving through removing the cause of the problem.

Now we come to the direct search for the truth.

We need to return to the cave analogy of Plato, which I shall repeat here for convenience. A person is chained up in a cave in such a manner that the person can only look at the back wall of the cave. Someone wanders into the cave. The chained-up person cannot turn around to see the newcomer but can see only the shadow of the newcomer projected on to the back wall of the cave by a fire at the mouth of the cave. Similarly as we go through life we cannot see the 'truth': we only see shadows or reflections of it. However, it is a fundamental belief that somewhere there is this deep truth, and we have to search for it.

Before Plato, philosophers like Parmenides and Heraclitus had been wrestling (not unlike the theatrical show wrestling that goes on today) with the problem of change. Heraclitus believed that all was change: you could never step into the 'same' river twice. Parmenides believed that there was an unchanging inner core. Plato put both these views together with his theory of 'inner forms' or 'essence'. Those were absolute and fixed while the surface stuff could change.

It should also be remembered that the scepticism and relativism of the sophists had made 'perception' dominant. Truth was what any man happened to perceive or believe. Truth was a matter of opinion, which meant that people and government could be persuaded by the skilled persuaders being trained by the sophists. We cannot be sure which came first: whether the teaching profession of the sophists necessitated this belief or whether the profession of teaching rhetoric arose, logically, from this belief.

It was on to this chaotic intellectual world that the fascist inclinations of Plato sought to impose order. There was an absolute and ultimate truth even if we could not see it. Because it was there, we ought to seek for it. The circularity of this particular 'belief system' has the key ingredients of any successful religious system (such as Freud's).

Underlying the varied surface appearance there was a similarity in things. Underlying the variations in a wide range of moggies there was an essential 'catness'. You could look at a variety of triangles with sides and angles of great difference, but underlying them all there was the ultimate form of a 'triangle'.

It must also be mentioned that Plato was strongly influenced by Pythagoras, the mathematician and mystic, who was describing universal mathematical truths – one of which every schoolchild learns to this day (Pythagoras's theorem about right-angled triangles). Just as there seemed to be ultimate truths in mathematics, so there must be in all things – if only we could discover them. Argument by analogy was the key form of argument for the Gang of Three.

Of course, Plato was partly right. Today we know that the gene structure of any cat is fundamentally the same, so it is no surprise that there is an underlying 'catness'. What Plato called the inner form of cats we might call the gene structure. In a different way, all tables have an underlying 'tableness', because if you order a table from a carpenter then the carpenter will seek to make a 'table' which is recognizable as such.

At points in the Socratic dialogues, Socrates emphasizes that the 'seen' is always changing but the 'unseen' (inner form) never changes. Plato insists that the only reason we can see or recognize a cat is that in our minds there is a permanent form of 'catness' and in every cat we see a projection of that form (like the shadow on the wall of the cave).

From this innate permanence of forms arises the notion that knowledge is only 'recollection' or the bringing into view of forms which have always been there. In the *Phaedo*, Socrates uses this notion directly as an argument for immortality. If knowledge is recollection then that knowledge must have been put in place in a previous life. Or, at least, the soul must have pre-existed. This notion of 'soul' very easily, via Paul, becomes the concept of the Christian soul.

In the dialogues, written by Plato, Socrates asks that his listeners assume that there is 'an absolute beauty and goodness' and that it is only by participating in this absolute beauty that beautiful things become beautiful. He challenges them to find how anything can come into existence 'other than by virtue of its own essence'.

So there is this belief that there is an inner truth which is hidden but which is absolute, ultimate, universal and unchanging. Now we set out to find it.

In contrast to the sophists, who doubted whether we could ever find such ultimate truths and who felt that we created our own, Socrates stoutly believed that the truth could be found by his method of inquiry. At the same time Socrates was convinced of his own ignorance and made a bit of a parade of that.

Socrates saw virtue as being the consequence of discovering knowledge and held that it was knowledge that students could be taught to discover.

So there was a top to the mountain – even if hidden in clouds. There were climbing techniques which could get us there and which we could learn. But Socrates was not himself the most fit of climbers and was conscious of his rather feeble efforts at climbing – or so he said.

It was on this basis that Socrates claimed to be only the 'midwife' who would bring forth the 'truth' from the minds in which it was already present but hidden.

Why should Socrates bother with midwifing the truth? Because he believed that discovery of the truth would improve human behaviour. His fundamental belief was that 'knowledge is virtue' and that a man who has full knowledge can do no wrong. So he fully agreed with the sophists that virtue could be improved through 'teachers and teaching' but, while they held that virtue could be taught more or less directly, Socrates saw virtue as being the consequence of discovering knowledge and held that it was knowledge that students could be taught to discover. It is not at all surprising that this view – which is extremely limited and deficient – is the basis of education today.

From all of this come the benefits of the 'endless search and inquiry' which has given Western civilization its apparent progress in general and certain progress in science and technology. Quite rightly we credit this search habit to Socrates and the Gang of Three. The notion that there is an ultimate truth and that we can seek to get nearer and nearer to that truth is what has driven science along. We must give boundless praise to the energy of that habit, with only the tiniest of complaints that the one area where we have not applied this endless search is to the very method itself.

Anyone who has seen the beautiful and amazing display of 'fractals' on a computer screen finds it very hard to believe that they have been generated by working through a simple mathematical relationship. In that case we start with the simple relationship and then find how astonishing and complex the results can be. In the endless search of science we start at the other end. We look at the complex results in the belief that at the end there will be the simplest of 'ultimate truths', like the simple mathematics that generates the fractals.

It is most ironic that, although Socrates and his fellows disdained science as pointless and considered it a waste of time (also reflected in traditional educational views), the most beneficial effects of his legacy have in fact been in the field of science.

But Socrates, himself, sought to make ethics, politics and other social matters the subject of his scientific inquiry. He hoped to discover universal laws and truths (as in mathematics) which would put these subjects on an absolute basis and so rescue them from the manipulation of people like the sophists.

Interestingly, Aristotle thought differently. Aristotle, the third member of the Gang of Three, wanted to distinguish between 'accuracy' or truth in studying science and 'practicality' in studying human behaviour. Aristotle did not fully believe that knowledge would automatically lead to virtue. He was interested less in 'knowing virtue' than in helping people to become 'virtuous'. In a strange way he was saying that science is a linear system but human behaviour is non-linear. It is only in the last 20 years or so, after centuries, that mathematics has finally accepted that much of the world is actually non-linear (with complex interactions and feedback loops, self-organizing systems, etc.).

We can extend this observation of Aristotle's to our general dealing with human behaviour.

The Freud model has been to dig deep and to seek to understand the underlying processes. 'What is really going on?' 'What is the real cause of this behaviour?' At times, however, we are forced to ask whether we are really discovering the deep truth or simply imposing a story – which may be just as therapeutic. If it is the latter then we come closer to the Eastern approach or even the Confucian approach which laid out behaviour patterns. Indeed some of the more recent trends in psychotherapy have been away from the 'deep-truth' discovery model to the cognitive-therapy approach which seeks to provide the person with a practical way of looking at the world and thinking about it. This deals directly with behaviour, unlike the Socratic route through 'knowledge of the truth'.

On the other hand, in schizophrenia the deep-truth search for the responsible gene and a possible chemical defect may eventually lead to a major improvement in treatment. Meanwhile the 'surface' approach seeks to make life more liveable for those suffering from schizophrenia.

There has always been a marked contrast between the East and the West with regard to deep and surface truth. The West has maintained that man should be judged by his 'soul' or inner truth. The East has been concerned more with the surface and prefers to judge people on their 'behaviour' in society and in their families. In the West 'honour' is some inner value, in the East honour is visible only in 'honourable behaviour'.

There is a big difference between 'deep massage' and 'surface massage'.

14 THE TRUTH

We come now to that most marvellously versatile and conveni-ent con trick called 'the truth'. Of course, if truth did not exist then the previous statement could never be true. Garlic exists but you do not seek to put garlic into everything that is cooked, such as chocolate cake.

Everyone knows that 'nature' is good. Everyone knows that all 'natural' things must be 'good' because they partake of that convenient label of value. But the most deadly poisons in the world are natural. Bacteria are natural, and so are viruses.

What is the most practical definition of the truth? Wherever you can apply the comment 'not so' then the opposite is the truth. In general, truth exists as the opposite of 'untruth', which is the real reality.

Truth is the key component of the fascist order which Plato successfully imposed on Western thinking. The children of truth are right and righteousness, and these in turn breed judgement, exclusion and inclusion, which in turn breed both persecution and progress.

If you find the taste of lettuce bitter then lettuce is bitter for you. That is the truth. But is lettuce bitter in an absolute sense? We could possibly derive some chemical definition of bitterness and test lettuce against it. We could possibly ask 1,000 people for their opinion and use the majority view as the 'truth'.

If, in an optical illusion, you see a line as 'curved' then you see that line as curved. No one can tell you otherwise. But you can lay a straight ruler against the line and show that it is not curved at all but straight. You can hide part of the optical illusion and now you see the line as straight. Unlike in the case of the lettuce, there is now an objective test of 'truth'.

As I have written in a preceding section, the sophists focused on perceptual truth. Gorgias, one of the sophists, claimed that there was no permanent truth 'but only what we can be persuaded to believe'. Protagoras claimed that 'man was the measure of all things' so man's perceptions created the truth.

It was against this background that Plato came up with his magnificent device of 'the absolute inner truth'. This was no longer subject to individual perceptual choice. Nor was it relative to circumstances. That belief has dominated Western thinking, and culture, ever since.

Truth is based far more on 'what is' than on 'what can be'.

It is not my intention in this book to proceed to a philosophical examination of truth as such. I am only interested in 'truth' as it affects our traditional thinking methods. Clearly 'truth' has a major impact on our thinking style and methods – which is why there has to be some consideration of the use of this thinking device.

Truth is the admittance label that allows things into your mind or into consideration. Truth is a party badge, a badge of membership. At the door everyone is checked. Only those with the truth label are allowed in; the rest are turned away. Then the thinker proceeds to organize those who have been allowed into the room.

The sophists immediately saw the flaw in this system. Truth or goodness are supposed to reside in the true or good thing (or person in the analogy). The sophists saw that this was non-sense. Mainly they saw this because, in those days, many of the thinkers had a medical background. In medicine something may be good for one illness but bad for another. The same substance may be wonderful in small quantities but poisonous in larger quantities. Protagoras pointed out that manure was good for plants if applied to the roots but damaging to young shoots. Obviously, goodness did not reside 'in' something but existed only in relation to something else. Hence the sophists were relativists.

Socrates was aware of this problem and defined 'goodness' in relation also to purpose. So a shuttle was good not only if it had the right shape but if it fulfilled the shuttle's purpose. But once we enter the 'system' world where do we draw the line? The shuttle is good for the loom. But is the loom good for society? The Luddites thought that the excellent mechanical loom was not good for society, because they were losing their jobs. But did the loss of those jobs matter, given the long-term availability of cheaper cloth? And so on.

I seem to be confusing 'truth' and 'goodness' here because that is precisely what did happen. The sophists were fed up with truth and preferred 'better' or 'worse' for some purpose or in some relationship. This is an extremely modern view. The Greek word '*kalos*' for beautiful seems to have meant 'fitting its purpose', and Socrates always seemed reluctant to abandon this notion in favour of Plato's more absolute 'truth as beauty'.

Wherever you can apply the comment 'not so' then the opposite is the truth.

The problem with the Socratic method and our thinking tra-dition is that we seek to proceed statement by statement. Is a particular statement true or false? But when we chop up complex systems into separate statements it is then impossible to make that judgement or, if it is made, it is likely to be incorrect in terms of the whole system. System relativity is sometimes essential. The atomistic, step-by-step process is simply inadequate. We cannot proceed by small steps each of which is soundly 'true'.

In practice we could possibly distinguish three broad types of truth. These types overlap greatly, because they are not designed as mutually exclusive boxes in the traditional way. (I shall deal later with the problem of 'hard-edged' boxes with judgement discriminations.)

1. Experience truth.
2. Game truth.
3. Belief truth.

Experience truth is based on our experience telling us that something 'is so'. If someone says something that is contrary to our experience, we say that it is 'not so'. Experience can be limited. If you have only experienced white swans you may be tempted to accept as true that all swans are white. Induction is a summary of available experience. Experience can be deceptive. Spanish settlers in South America thought that llamas came into season only at certain times. Later it turned out that, like rabbits, llamas are ready to mate whenever the male is around. Perceptual truth may be based on experience and may be deceived, as in the optical illusion.

The conclusions of science are based on general experience, as in observation, or special experience as in a designed experiment. This sort of truth is useful, pragmatic and progressive. It has its greatest value when we do not regard it as absolute but only as a 'proto-truth' which is valuable precisely because we are trying to change it.

Then there is game truth. If you play Monopoly, contract bridge, chess or go (the Japanese board game) you follow the rules because those rules are 'true' for that game. If you invent a new game, as I did with the L-Game,* then you invent the rules yourself. When you are playing that game you use those rules. Mathematics is a prime example of a game truth. No one would attempt to argue that 2 + 2 does not equal 4. But even mathematics is limited to a particular universe in which it was set up (in spherical geometry, parallel lines do meet). Mathematics is a game truth through which we can look at the world in order to get some experience truths.

What Plato and the Gang of Three did was to create a game truth, to impose this on the world, and then to pretend that it was an experience truth which was there to be discovered. They would argue that their attempt was really the same as that of mathematics. Which it was.

If you measure a table and find that the surface is one metre from the floor, is this experience truth or game truth? There is a game in which we have a ruler with numbers on it. We place this ruler against the table and read off the number, which says 100 centimetres. This is the game with rulers and numbers. We do it over and again and the result is always the same. This is experience.

Belief truth is the most powerful of them all, because it is the one which enters our minds and works therein. A belief truth is what we have come to believe. It may be directly related to reality or it may not. We may believe that the table is always going to measure one metre. That is a belief. Plato's notion of absolute inner truths was a belief system which was imposed on the intellectual world. Freud's view of the importance of childhood trauma is a belief system. We could never survive without an intricate repertoire of belief truths.

Belief truths are most important because they structure life, provide values and make decisions easier. The key question is:

* See my book *The Five-Day Course in Thinking* (London: Penguin, 1970).

How firmly do we hold these belief truths? There is the tentative belief truth which is a hypothesis. The hypothesis is what has really driven Western scientific progress. Hypotheses are valuable and powerful. They create frames for looking and frames for organizing. But what about other belief truths? Should they also be tentative? If people want stability and certainty, are tentative belief truths going to be much value? Here we might circle back to game truth. If we want to set up our values and world view in a particular way and wish to play that game then there can be the certainty of game truth. This is what Plato and the Gang of Three were really about in their world view: a belief truth changed into a game truth and then supposed to be an experience truth.

As far as the brain is concerned, truth is probably always circular. You conceive a 'possibility' then you check the outer world to confirm your guess.

What is the practical value of 'truth' for thinking?

The belief that there is a deep truth to be discovered leads to the endless search for it.

Truth is a label that is easily attached by judgement. This in turn leads to acceptance or rejection. This can have a profound effect on our thinking behaviour, as I shall attempt to describe in later sections.

The hard-edged dichotomy of true/false pushes things one way or the other when they might better be in the middle.

True/false judgement allows the operation of the 'box' system of categories, with its rigid inflexibility.

The true/false step-by-step sequence can be misleading and deceptive in the hands of those who want to misuse it.

The truth label permits a permanent classification which rarely gets re-examined.

'Truth' becomes an easy justification for actions and beliefs ranging from persecutions to racism.

Truth is a powerful banner behind which to rally people.

Truth is a powerful weedkiller to cut down nonsenses.

Truth puts into solid permanence what we want to believe at the moment.

Absolute truth overrides the reality of complex system interactions.

Truth sets out to map the world in a usable way.

Truth is based far more on 'what is' than on 'what can be'.

Truth favours analysis rather than design.

Design

Analysis

Truth favours description rather than creativity.

Truth preserves paradigms instead of changing them.

Truth makes judgement all-important.

Truth encourages destructive judgement rather than constructive effort.

Truth leads to smugness, complacency and arrogance.

Truth gives us confidence.

Truth is an attack weapon.

Truth allows us to say 'not so' both when this is justified and when it is not.

However we look at it, this notion of 'truth' is the keystone of the Socratic method and the traditional Western thinking system put together by the Gang of Three.

What is the alternative?

Humility...

Possibly.

Maybe.

That is one way of looking at it.

In those circumstances.

It serves its purpose.

'Not proven' (as in the Scottish legal system).

Both yes and no.

It seems so.

Sometimes.

Would we really suffer from this sort of 'floppiness'? Could a judge say: 'The jury [or some other means] has assessed that there is a 10 per cent chance of your being guilty so I am going to give you 10 per cent of the sentence'? Probably not. But a pre-court hearing could say: 'There is a 10 per cent chance of your being guilty so you go to the fast-action court rather than waiting months for the full-action court.'

15 QUESTIONS

If we have now come to believe, as Plato would wish us to, that there is an inner, hidden, unchanging truth, how are we going to find it? Now that we have a 'destination', how are we going to get there?

As I have suggested, there seem to be two fundamental approaches. The first approach is to reject the 'untruth', the false ideas, the incorrect thinking and the nonsenses. The second approach is to go more directly towards that truth/Truth.

One of the key tools of the second approach is the 'question'. The endless inquiry set up by the belief in a hidden truth is to be carried out largely by questions. If truth is the top of the mountain then the 'question' is one of the basic climbing techniques we need to use in order to get there.

Most people know that the basis of the Socratic method is the 'question'. Socrates's barrage of questions seemed to have irritated those who did not love him. He did not provide many answers, but his questions came in quick-fire order.

The irony, as I have pointed out in a preceding section, is that Socrates himself did not really use the Socratic method.

Anyone who reads the Socratic dialogues (as written by Plato) is at once struck by the lack of real questions. Socrates makes statement after statement. And after each statement he turns to the listener and says: 'Is that not so?' The sort of responses that are given include:

'Yes.'

'True.'

'Certainly.'

'Quite so.'

'It is as you say.'

'Definitely not' (when asked to confirm a negative).

'I would say so.'

'I agree.'

In the *CoRT Thinking Lessons*,[*] I suggest that there are two types of question: the 'shooting question' and the 'fishing question'.

When a hunter shoots at something, he or she knows exactly what he or she is aiming at. The target is already known. The hunter may hit or the hunter may miss. The two possible outcomes are known in advance. So with 'shooting questions' we know the basic answers in advance. The answer will be either a 'yes' or a 'no'.

'Is it Wednesday today?'

'Is Sweden a member of the European Union?'

'Is this leaf good to eat?'

'Is that direction [pointing] north?'

The questioner is seeking to check something out. The questioner wants a 'possibility' affirmed or denied. In the game of 'Twenty Questions' the player has to identify an object by asking a series of shooting questions:

'Is it an animal?'

'Does it have four legs?'

---

[*] A 60-lesson programme used for the direct teaching of thinking as a curriculum subject. Published by Perfection Learning 1000 North Second Avenue, Logan, Iowa 51546, USA.

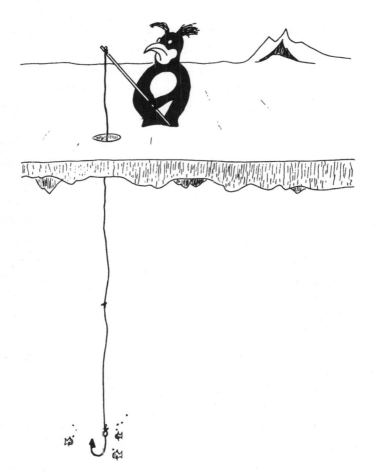

'Can it usually be found in houses?'

'Does it like eating mice?'

The 'fishing question' is different. The fisherman puts bait on the hook and sits down to 'await' what might happen. The fisherman is not 'aiming' at a particular fish (though this is occasionally the case in a river pool) but putting down bait and waiting to see what is attracted to it. The fisherman may know the broad type of fish that will be caught. If you go fishing for blue marlin you are not likely to catch a trout. A 'fishing question' is a searching question rather than a 'checking-out' question.

'What day is it today?'

'Who are the members of the European Union?'

'Which leaves around here are good to eat?'

'Where is the north?'

The person replying to a 'fishing question' must do more than offer a 'yes' or a 'no'. The reply has to have content.

Now Socrates often asked his listeners for proposed definitions (of morality, love, justice, etc.) but the bulk of his questioning was of the shooting type. In fact, it was not even of the normal shooting type, where the questioner is not really sure whether the answer is going to be 'yes' or 'no'. Socrates fully expected the answer to be a definite 'yes'. He fully expected agreement. He would probably have been very put out if the answer had been 'no' or 'maybe'. So we have to ask whether these were really questions at all or a monologue punctuated at times by a request for assent. I am not suggesting that there is anything wrong with such a monologue: merely that the open questioning we often associate with the Socratic method was rarely used by Socrates himself (at least as written up by Plato).

Questions are a most useful language device. As far as I know, most languages use the question device – I would be most interested to hear of those that do not. We may wonder how we could manage without the 'question'.

Most people make the mistake of believing that because something is simple, obvious and sensible we do it all the time.

Think of some possible questions:

'How old are you?'

'What do you think of Malta as a holiday place?'

'How would you like your fried eggs cooked?'

'Are you deaf?'

Next, consider how you could convey exactly the same meaning without using the question device at all. At first this may seem difficult, but actually it is extremely easy.

'Direct your attention to your age. Tell me your age.'

'Direct your attention to Malta as a holiday place. Share your thoughts with me.'

'Direct your attention to the cooking of your fried eggs. Indicate to me your preferred style.'

This last question usually disturbs visitors to the USA who assume that fried eggs are 'fried eggs'. In fact you are required to indicate whether you want your fried eggs 'over easy', 'sunny side up' or some other possibility.

In more extreme cases the final question may better be done with sign language (if you believe the other person is really deaf). You point at your ear and make a gesture. Pointing at your ear is the equivalent of saying: 'Direct your attention to your ear.'

In each of the examples given, the phrase 'Direct your attention to ...' is cumbersome and really unnecessary. You could just as simply say: 'Tell me your age.' I have, however, included the phrase because it is always implicit.

A question is a device for 'directing attention' to a particular matter and asking the listener to recount what he or she 'sees'.

A tourist guide in front of a cathedral might say:

'Direct your attention to that large window above the door. Tell me what you see.'

'Direct your attention to the buttresses. Tell me what you notice.'

'Direct your attention to the carving at the top of that pillar. Tell me what you see.'

It is obviously impossible to look at everything at once, so 'attention-directing' devices are most useful. There are various phrases which can carry out this 'attention-directing' function:

'Tell me about ...'

'Direct your attention to ...'

'Look at ...'

'Focus upon ...'

But, on the whole, the question is the preferred device because it is more polite (asking instead of instructing) and simpler to use.

Attention-directing is a very important part of perception. An expert in a subject may have acquired an 'attention-directing framework'. When an art expert looks at a painting, that expert may direct his or her attention to the colours, the brushwork, the composition, the use of light, the hands, etc. A hypothesis will itself immediately direct attention. If the expert believes that the unsigned work is by a certain artist then the expert may immediately look at the nose because that artist is known to paint noses in a characteristic way.

In thinking about anything we need 'attention-directing' frameworks. We cannot look at everything at the same time in order to put us into the same position as an expert who has built up just such a framework. We need attention-directing devices in order to prevent confusion. It is more effective to look at one thing after another and to make a thorough job of each 'look'.

We also need attention-directing devices in order to be sure that we have not left anything out but have done a broad and competent perceptual scan: that we have looked in all directions that matter.

The *CoRT Thinking Lessons,* which are now in wide use in many countries around the world and with excellent results, deliberately provide just such attention-directing devices.

So instead of the hit-and-miss haphazard questioning of the Socratic method we can have the organized attention-directing of the 'de Bono method' of parallel thinking.

The formal attention-directing devices of the CoRT method provide 'executive concepts' for the mind. Our minds are full of 'descriptive concepts' like chair, car, dog, etc. But there are few, if any, executive concepts, which we use to direct our thinking or attention.

In the CoRT lessons there is an attention-directing device called 'C&S'. This stands for 'Consequence and Sequel' but is always referred to by the initials. Why? To give it its own perceptual identity. It is perfectly useless simply to exhort someone to 'look at the consequences'. Such an instruction, which would apparently do the same thing, has no permanent standing in the mind, whereas the C&S comes to have its own identity. When a teacher asks a student to 'do a C&S' the student knows exactly what to do. In time the student gives himself or herself the same instruction. The results, as shown by the research of Professor John Edwards at James Cook University in Australia, can be very powerful.

Just telling a student to 'think' is perfectly useless.

In Canada I once suggested to a roomful of about 150 senior women executives that women should be paid 15 per cent more money than men for doing the same job. Eighty per cent of those present liked the idea and even muttered that it was 'about time too'. I then briefly explained the C&S technique: direct attention to immediate, short-term, medium-term and long-term consequences of the suggestion. At the end I again asked for their opinion regarding the suggestion. The 80 per cent in favour had now dropped to only 15 per cent. So 'doing a formal C&S' had made a huge difference. Now, I suspect that everyone in that room would have regarded the C&S as an unnecessary device because as 'thinking adults' they always looked at the consequences of a suggestion. If so then the formal request to do a C&S should have made no difference at all.

Most people make the mistake of believing that because something is simple, obvious and sensible we do it all the time. This is not so at all. We do not usually do even the simplest of things.

I have often told how I once asked a class of 30 12-year-olds in a school in Australia to give me their reaction to the suggestion that they should each receive a small amount of money each week for going to school. All 30 thought it was a great idea since they would be able to buy sweets, comics and chewing gum. I then briefly explained another simple attention-directing device: the 'PMI'. Here the thinker directs attention to the 'plus' points first, followed by the 'minus' points and finally the 'interesting' points. At the end of the exercise 29 of the 30 students had totally changed their mind and decided that the suggestion was a bad idea: 'Where would the money come from?', etc. The important point to notice about this story is that I did not stand there asking them questions. I did not say another word after explaining the PMI. The students used this attention-directing device on their own. As a result, they had a broader perceptual picture. As a result of having a broader perceptual picture they changed their mind about the suggestion. The difference from the Socratic method, in which the teacher has to ask a string of questions, is very obvious.

Other attention-directing tools in the first set of *CoRT Thinking Lessons* include:

CAF: Consider All Factors – this directs attention to all the
   factors that need to be looked at when considering a decision,
   choice, design, plan, etc.
FIP: First Important Priorities – an attempt to spell out the
   priorities. Which things matter most?
AGO: Aims, Goals and Objectives – this directs attention to
   the purpose of the action or choice. What are you trying
   to achieve?
APC: Alternatives, Possibilities and Choices – this is an
   executive order to find other ways of looking at something
   or doing something.
OPV: Other People's Views – this directs attention to the
   view or thinking of the other people involved.

All these attention-directing devices are very obvious and very simple. But, in action, they have a powerful effect. And students love using them, because they provide a framework for thinking about something. Just telling a student to 'think' is perfectly useless.

One enlightened philosopher in Canada declared that the devices could not possibly work. Even as he was writing this the devices were in use in hundreds of classrooms, where they were working very well. It is somewhat like trying to prove that cheese does not exist when people are eating cheese every day.

We get many reports of children going home and teaching the attention-directing devices to their parents who are about to make major decisions. We get reports of children helping their fathers and mothers think through business decisions. There are countries where the methods are taught in some, many or all the schools.

There is no magic. A question is an attention-directing device. But who tells you where to direct the question? The CoRT thinking tools provide a framework for directing the directing of attention. The CoRT method also gets the students or thinkers to direct their own attention instead of just waiting for the teacher to ask the right question.

The *CoRT Thinking Lessons* are also used in business as well as in schools.

Childwall Library

Title: When bad things happen in good bikinis :
life after death and a dog called B
ID: 9350391798
Due: 13/03/2020 23:59

Title: country doctor's choice
ID: 9336520950
Due: 13/03/2020 23:59

Title: Confidence : transform the way you feel
so you can achieve the things you wa
ID: 9336124648
Due: 13/03/2020 23:59

Title: I'm ok, you're ok
ID: 9350662341
Due: 13/03/2020 23:59

Title: Parallel thinking : from Socratic to de
Bono thinking
ID: 9350246100
Due: 13/03/2020 23:59

Title: Why walk when you can fly? : how to soar
beyond your fears and embrace your
ID: 9333519919
Due: 13/03/2020 23:59

Total items: 6
21/02/2020 12:10
Checked out: 9

FWS1

Childwall Library

Title: When bad things happen in good bikinis :
life after death and a dog called B
ID: 93503917 98
Due: 13/03/2020 23:59

Title: country doctor's choice
ID: 93365520950
Due: 13/03/2020 23:59

Title: Confidence : transform the way you feel
so you can achieve the things you wa
ID: 93361246 48
Due: 13/03/2020 23:59

Title: I'm ok, you're ok
ID: 93506652341
Due: 13/03/2020 23:59

Title: Parallel thinking : from Socratic to de
Bono thinking
ID: 93502461 00
Due: 13/03/2020 23:59

Title: Why walk when you can fly? : how to soar
beyond your fears and embrace your
ID: 93335159 19
Due: 13/03/2020 23:59

Total items: 6
21/02/2020 12:10
Checked out: 9

Thank you for using Childwall Library. Renew
24/7 at www.liverpool.gov.uk/libraries or call
0151 233 3000.

FW51

16 DEFINITIONS, BOXES, CATEGORIES AND GENERALIZATIONS

Here we come to the very core of the Western thinking tradition, the very core of the Socratic method and the very core of the work of the Gang of Three. 'Truth' is determined by what is allowed into a particular box. Harsh judgement is to decide what (or who) is accepted into the box and what (or who) is not accepted. This basic concept of boxes has totally dominated Western thinking – sometimes with excellent effect and sometimes with disastrous effect. Is this 'belief system' (belief in boxes) inevitable or just one way of looking at the world?

Socrates set out to find absolute definitions. He demanded absolute definitions. He was not prepared to compromise, and would rather give up in failure, as he often did, than accept a pragmatic definition instead. Any single refutation of an attempted definition was enough to destroy that definition.

This attitude of Socrates was determined by his 'mission'. At the time he lived, words like 'justice', 'virtue', 'morality' were used very casually. People gave these words whatever meaning they needed for their persuasive efforts, just as politicians do to this day. The sophists believed in expediency and personal perceptual truth. The sophists also taught the art of persuasion, which allowed people to mould words to their expedient meaning. It was into this highly elastic world that Socrates crusaded with his mission to find absolute and unchanging definitions. Expediency was out.

Socrates wanted universal standards, forms, definitions and principles. Socrates was seeking the '*logos*' of a situation in its definition. The definition was to lay out the essential nature of something and the factors which were constant when other aspects varied.

Aristotle took all this much further. Aristotle regarded the main contribution of Socrates to science to be his search for definitions. He declared that there were two things which should properly be credited to Socrates:

1. Inductive argument.
2. General definitions.

A lot of thinking at the time of Socrates was contributed by medical people, who had to combine science, philosophy and practical action. It is unfortunate today that philosophy is left to philosophers, who do not have that need for practical action.

Illness was regarded as the invasion of an 'evil spirit'. So it was important to try to identify the nature (Aristotle later called it the '*eidos*') of the illness. This identification or diagnosis allowed the doctor to know which standard action to apply. Here was a direct and practical need to move from classification to action. To this day we still give 'names' to diseases. This has probably impeded the progress of medicine, because it diverts attention from the cross-system nature of illness.

Socrates is rightly credited with providing the basis for classification in science. Certain branches of science – botany, for example – depend heavily on classification. Unfortunately, there are other scientists who feel that science is all about classification. In the USA there is a strong tendency in psychology to put people into classes, groups, classifications, categories and boxes. Tests are devised for this purpose and are administered with proper scientific solemnity. Very little of practical value comes out of this exercise. People are put into their boxes and stay there. It is only too easy to devise reliable tests to put people into boxes of any sort. Indeed, people are only too anxious to put themselves in boxes as a form of self-knowledge. Hence the interest in astrological and zodiac 'boxing'.

Procrustes is said to have had but one bed for his guests. A guest who was too long or too short was 'trimmed' or 'adjusted' to fit the bed. That is one of the more obvious dangers of forcing people into boxes. Selective perception can do a good job of trimming people to fit a chosen box.

A definition is a clustering together of necessary features. Socrates had a hard time trying to decide whether the definition of bravery should include or exclude knowledge. Let us have a look at the problem.

1. A person who does not know that bullets can kill is not really brave when he charges over the top of a trench.
2. When the person has more knowledge and knows that bullets kill then it is bravery that makes him advance.
3. If the person has good statistical knowledge that the chances of being hit are only 1 in 200 then the bravery diminishes again.
4. If the person knows that even a slight wound is likely to be serious under battlefield conditions then bravery increases again.
5. If the person knows that the attack is only a decoy and will be recalled soon then the bravery diminishes again.
6. If the person knows that his chance of surviving until the end of the year is very low (as it was for officers in the First World War) then the bravery increases again.

So is knowledge part of the definition of bravery or not? The problem is that some knowledge makes for bravery and some knowledge diminishes bravery. That is one of the classic problems of definitions and category judgements.

If the brain were to be a more efficient device we would be much less efficient as thinkers.

Socrates used boxes very skilfully, as suggested in Figure 4. He would get a listener to agree that he was comfortable in one box. Then Socrates would show that this led on to another box. And then another box. So step by step the listener was painlessly transported to a position that he (usually) might never have chosen in the first place. This is exactly the reasoning that skilled lawyers use in court.

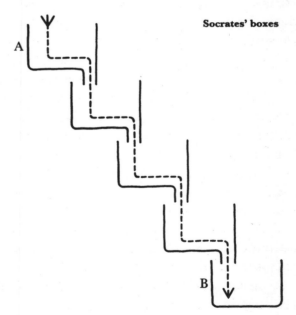

Socrates' boxes

Figure 4

I have never really understood why philosophers have always made such a heavy meal of definitions, categories and boxes.

I suspect it is all to do with the underlying notion of absolute truth and the need to have 'is' and 'is not'. The boxes have hard edges, and something has to be definitely in or definitely out.

Yet a definition could be seen as a clustering of attributes which we usually find together and therefore expect to find together. There is nothing very hard about that. Because we have usually come across these attributes together, we have a certain expectation to find them together. This is exactly how a doctor proceeds in diagnosing an illness from certain symptoms and tests. Not all the symptoms may be present, but the doctor makes a probabilistic guess.

It is when this sort of probabilistic guess becomes a hard-edged certainty that the trouble starts. Aristotle possibly knew that stallions had more teeth than mares. So he held it as a certainty that the male of any species has more teeth than the female. He claimed this and never bothered to ask either of his two wives to open their mouths to count their teeth.

Why is it not enough to say that swans are usually white and so we expect a swanlike creature to be white? This is an expectation based on our current experience. But it does not have to be a hard-edged definition, and when we discover that there are black swans we can still hold on to that 'usually'.

The difficulty is that we are then dealing with a probabilistic system which can no longer be operated on the sharp true/false basis. It now becomes very difficult to 'exclude' things. Above all, where is the 'inner truth'?

Some classes are based on 'inner truths' – for example gene structures or the simple mathematical basis for a fractal. Others are clusters of convenience.

With what I call 'game truth' there is no problem at all, because you decide the basis for a grouping.

'I am going to call every woman with blonde hair a blonde.' Obviously there are no exceptions, because an exception would not be called a blonde. Then you might wish to go beyond appearance (why?) to differentiate between genetic blondes and cultured blondes.

Authority truth

But Socrates was not using 'game truth'. He wanted to arrive at his definition by induction from experience and examples. He would have been far better off with 'game truth' and deciding what the definition was to be – as in promulgating a law. But then where would his authority have come from? In believing, sincerely, that he was finding the inner truth, he then derived authority from that truth.

In my early example of the grammarians trying to derive rules from current usage there would usually come a point where, in frustration, they would have to 'create' a rule which covered most usage but excluded some as 'incorrect usage'. Socrates did not want to do that.

Imagine two hawks. One hawk has excellent eyesight but the other hawk is somewhat short-sighted. The hawks live on a diet of frogs, mice and lizards. The keen-sighted hawk can identify a frog from a great height and so decides his menu in advance. He prefers frogs and only eats frogs. He forgets about other possible foods. The short-sighted hawk cannot do this, so this hawk creates a concept, class or category of 'small things that move'. When this hawk is hungry and sees a 'small thing that moves' the hawk dives – not knowing exactly what is on the menu. Sometimes the hawk finds a mouse, sometimes a frog, sometimes a lizard and sometimes even a child's toy. Clearly the first hawk is in a better position because of his good eyesight. Not so. Suppose the frogs die out – perhaps through overindulgence by the hawks (like overfishing). The first hawk is in trouble. With the short-sighted hawk the demise of the frogs makes very little difference. Classes, categories and concepts can give flexibility.

It could even be argued that it is the 'internal short-sightedness' of the human brain which makes its 'blurry vision' so very useful for thinking. If the brain were to be a more efficient device we would be much less efficient as thinkers.

From where do concepts and 'inner forms' come?

The Platonic view is that they are already present in our minds – possibly from the pre-existence of the soul, as Socrates argued.

Then there is the 'averaging' view. This holds that after we have seen a variety of cats we develop a sort of overlapped 'average' concept of a cat. It is now claimed that neural-network computers can actually form such 'concepts' from overlapped experience.

This basic concept of boxes has totally dominated Western thinking – sometimes with excellent effect and sometimes with disastrous effect.

There is a third view. This view holds that the first exposure to a cat imprints a large and vague representation of a cat in the mind. On to this come later, more specific, details of cats. This first-formed blurry image remains the 'concept' of the cat.

Categories are there for the convenience of action, as in the diagnosis of a doctor. Categories are also there for discrimination and for sorting things out, as in scientific inquiry. The trouble arises when we mix up game truth and experience truth, convenience categories and 'inner-truth' categories, and treat them all as if they are 'inner-truth' categories arising from experience.

It could be argued that racism and persecution come from the harsh judgements that arise from hard-edged categories. This would probably be unfair, because category hatreds are common in cultures which have not had this 'inner-truth' belief system. Nevertheless, this natural human tendency to categorize, box and judge may be enhanced and given apparent justification by the traditional Western thinking system.

What is the alternative? What does parallel thinking have to offer at this point? A move towards probabilistic systems and fuzzy logic. Instead of boxes there would be flagpoles around which attributes gather, as I suggested in a much earlier book.* Instead of 'always' and 'never' we might come to use 'usually', 'by and large' and 'rarely'. In most cases, I believe, this would be a big improvement – once we had got used to it. We might still reserve the hard-edged boxes for certain aspects of scientific research when linear systems are being studied, though I even have my doubts about that.

I shall be dealing with the important matter of 'hard-edged' boxes in a later section.

* *De Bono's Thinking Course* (London: 2006).

17 THE VALUE OF BOXES

The value of systematic filing is that you are going to find what you expect in each file. If you have a file for 'Unpaid Bills' then you are going to find unpaid bills in that file. What you put in is what you get out. The more accurate that you are in filing, the more accurate will be your retrieval and the more confidence you will have in your filing system.

The purpose of definitions, categories and boxes is to make sense of the world and to make it simpler. Instead of having to react to every individual item, we react to the broad grouping that comes under the 'file name'. A general category called 'snakes' will make us wary of all snakes. We do not have to check whether or not this particular one is dangerous or whether it happens to be in a bad mood.

Boxes make the world easier to look at and easier to deal with. We can now predict behaviour. A doctor can predict that a person in a hypoglycaemic coma will react well to being given sugar. A doctor can predict that the streptococcus germ will be killed by penicillin.

Adjectives are powerful boxes. They are boxes themselves and not just labels attached to other boxes. The adjective 'unpleasant' puts everything to which that adjective is attached into a box along with all other things that most people 'would not find pleasing'. Beware of anyone who uses a lot of adjectives: the chances are that that person cannot think. This is particularly true of journalists who slip in adjectives as substitutes for thoughts.

Then there are the really big boxes which are so useful for bringing up children: 'good', 'bad', 'right', 'wrong', 'true', 'false', etc. It is enough to slap on one of these big labels to indicate that 'something should be done' or 'something should not be done'. Why it should or should not be done, or under what circumstances, are not explained, because that would take up too much time and be too complex. A parent can tell a child that 'red berries are bad for you' without having to identify every poisonous red berry botanically and without having to explain the intricacies of specialized chemistry and physiology.

If a child asks 'why' such berries are bad, the parent may bring out a more specific box: 'because they will make you sick'. A child knows what 'being sick' means, so there is no need to go into further details.

'Men are brutal and selfish exploiters of women.'

This can be simplified to 'Men are brutes.' Many people would object and would argue that 'Some men are brutes.' Does this mean that these brutish men are brutal all the time? Or do they behave brutally now and then?

Perhaps it is not the boxes that are the problem but the arrogant, absolute certainty with which we hold a particularly boxed view of the world.

Should we perhaps say: 'Some men are brutes when they are behaving brutally'? That may have a high descriptive value but it does not have much predictive value. We can get around this problem by using the concept of 'potentially'. So we might feel happier saying: 'Men are potentially brutes.' We are still left with a problem. Is the potential high? Should we regard all men as being likely brutes? If the potential is thought to be too low then we may not be sufficiently on guard against brutish behaviour. We would dearly like to have a more precise discriminating factor on our box label: 'Men with small noses are brutes.' I have no evidence that is true, but such a discriminator would allow us to increase our level of wariness with certain men.

The whole purpose of experience, information and science is to seek out more and more specific boxes. We need to get ever more exact in our recognition and prediction. Doctors no longer treat 'diabetes' as a single illness-box but distinguish different types of diabetes with different mechanisms, treatments and predictions. At the same time as we are seeking smaller and more specific boxes we are also seeking larger boxes in the form of universal laws or principles. The dual process of 'splitting' (more specific boxes) and 'lumping' (bigger boxes) goes on all the time in science. In science the lumping process is an attempt to find universal laws. In life the lumping process is an attempt to simplify the world and to provide a convenient focus for emotions – as in racism.

Could we live without the simplifying convenience of 'boxes'? Probably not, on a personal level, though in the future computers will allow us to make much better statistical (probability) assessments. Do boxes give rise to a dangerous way of looking at the world? In some cases they undoubtedly do so but we could not 'abolish' boxes on those grounds, because of their high value elsewhere.

So where does that leave us?

We can avoid the too easy use of adjectives. We can avoid large generalizations. We can challenge assumptions and sloppy definitions – just as Socrates set out to do. But Socrates challenged existing definitions in his search for the 'true' definition. At this point we part company with Socrates. Perhaps it is not the boxes that are the problem but the arrogant, absolute certainty with which we hold a particularly boxed view of the world.

18 THE PROBLEM OF 'IS'

Socrates set out on his 'endless inquiry' in search of the truth. Plato made sure, in his writings, that Socrates was searching for this 'truth'. It may be that in rea life Socrates was a bright fellow who built his reputation on challenging people's views and was not particularly concerned with finding some 'truth' but merely in showing that all assumptions could be attacked – and showing off as he did so. Nevertheless, the combined result of the Gang of Three was the idea that there was an absolute truth which was hidden and could be found. If there was no such truth, what was the point of endless inquiry?

We may repeat that question, because it is rather important for 'parallel' thinking. What is the point of endless inquiry if there is no ultimate truth to be found? We could provide some other reasons for endless inquiry.

We could search for 'better', 'more useful' or 'more convenient' ways of looking at things. This is more or less what the sophists like Protagoras did when they preferred terms like 'better' or 'worse' to 'truth'.

We could search for different ways of looking at things, in order to lay out alongside each other a number of such ways. This is the essence of parallel thinking. We seek to multiply the parallel ways of looking at things.

'Red berries are "bad" for you.'

'Red berries are poisonous.'

'People believe that red berries are poisonous.'

'Red berries look nice.'

'Red berries could taste nice.'

If we lay out these parallel possibilities, it is obvious that the downside of the 'danger' far exceeds the upside of the nice colour. So, as a practical decision, you do not eat the berries.

There is much too close a relation between 'is' and the 'truth'. When we put something into a box we do so with the absolute certainty that this is 'identification' of its true nature. We take the sort of truth that attaches to Pythagoras's theorem and we apply it to all our box identifications.

A law court cannot just admit the 'possibility' of guilt or 'suspend judgement'. For practical purposes the court has to decide whether an accused 'is' or 'is not' guilty.

Because of our need for practical action, because of our belief in 'truth', because of the cultural influence of the Gang of Three we believe that we need the certainty of 'is' in order to operate our box system.

Once the thinker has judged into which box something should go, that becomes the 'truth' and action is determined by the label on the box.

The point that concerned the sophists was that qualities such as 'good' or 'bad' resided not in things but only in systems. One person might be severely allergic to a substance that was harmless to everyone around. One type of treatment might be beneficial for one type of illness but very dangerous in another. All those involved in medicine knew this very well. How then could they judge something 'in itself'? This led to the concept of 'relativism' which Plato so abhorred. Through Socrates, he tried to deal with the problem by including a 'sense of purpose' in the definition of 'good'. But even this is weak. The purpose of wine is to taste good. But for a reformed alcoholic or for someone with cirrhosis, or even for someone who is going to have to drive home, wine may be bad even though it is fulfilling its purpose. If we enlarge 'purpose' to include the whole present and future well-being of that person then we are just giving relativity another name.

While the arrogant certainty of 'is' and identity may have given us the advantage of a fascist law and order in our thinking and may have been responsible for some progress, it has also been responsible for much misery and for holding back progress that depends on a more holistic 'systems' approach.

'Plato, in his writing, is a fascist. Therefore we should condemn him and his influence.' Many will argue as to whether or not he was a fascist or whether it is fair to apply this modern term to his well-meaning attempt to avoid the pitfalls of a rabble democracy. All such defence completely misses the point. There is no reason to condemn Plato because in his writings he is a fascist. Does this mean approval of what normally goes into the box labelled 'fascist'? Some might even argue that point. From my point of view, 'fascist' as a term of convenience is one possible way of looking at Plato's work because it covers the general attributes of absolutes, certainties, inclusion and exclusion, and the sort of imposed order that is found in fascism. There are, no doubt, parallel ways of looking at his work. Nor is there any reason to condemn Plato simply because of the normal reaction to the label 'fascist'. We simply go forward to look at the features of his world view and thinking system and examine the value and dangers of those: there are some 'plus' points, some 'minus' points and some 'interesting' points. We then proceed to see whether, at different points, we can improve or replace the methods he used.

At the more complex levels of thinking there is no doubt at all that we should be moving on to considering whole systems.

In the previous example we are concerned with 'moving forward', not with making judgements based on 'is'. This is the essential difference between 'rock logic', which is concerned with judgement and identification as the basis for action, and 'water logic', which moves forward to examine what follows. The key operating word in rock logic has always been 'is'. The key operating word in water logic is 'to': 'What does this lead "to"?' This overlaps with the pragmatism of the American philosopher William James, who was also unhappy with a philosophy based on identity rather than on the practicality of what happened next.

The 'to' of water logic leads on to relativity and the systems view.

While at the more complex levels of thinking there is no doubt at all that we should be moving on to considering whole systems, what about the day-to-day thinking of those who do not have the time to deal with whole systems at every moment? Surely the convenience and the certainty of the traditional 'arrogant' box system is more practical?

We find that youngsters who have learned the parallel thinking of the CoRT method at school take a much broader view (considering the consequences of action, other people's views, etc.) without any difficulty. Those who have learned the Six Hats method find that they can apply it to any situation.

The contrast is quite sharp.

In traditional thinking there is perception followed by a judgement which puts the matter into a box. Action is then determined by the box.

In parallel thinking there is perception which is enhanced by attention-directing frameworks. The result is a number of parallel considerations. These determine the design of action.

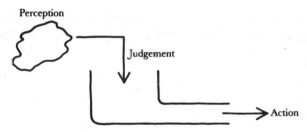

Traditional thinking

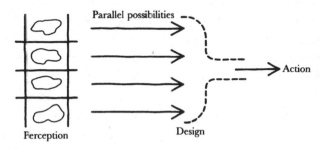

Figure 5   Parallel thinking

The contrast is shown in Figure 5.

The essential difference is that in the traditional method (the Socratic method, the Gang of Three, etc.) judgement is the key thinking step. Once the thinker has judged into which box something should go, that becomes the 'truth' and action is determined by the label on the box.

In the Socratic method, judgement is the key thinking operation.

In parallel thinking, 'exploration' is the key thinking operation.

In my view the total emphasis on 'critical thinking' in education is not only misguided but positively dangerous because it reinforces the notion that judgement ('critical' means 'judgement') is all that matters. This then means that we use the stereotype boxes that are so dangerous in society.

Of course, critical thinking is a useful part of thinking, just as the front left wheel is a useful part of the car. But we have to break the stranglehold that 'judgement' has acquired over Western thinking culture. It is only if we do this that we can develop the more flexible benefits of the exploration of parallel thinking.

19 THE TYRANNY OF JUDGEMENT

'*Does* your grandmother like carrots?'
  'Yes.'
'Does your grandmother like marrows?'
  'Yes.'
'Does your grandmother like peas?'
  'No.'
'Does your grandmother like tomatoes?'
  'No.'
'Does your grandmother like lettuce?'
  'Yes.'

So what vegetables does the grandmother like? That is a well-known children's game in which one person has to deduce the 'principle' on which the grandmother likes certain vegetables but not others. Here there is a 'true' principle to be discovered precisely because it has been put there (a matter of 'game truth').

Who has put there the principle that the three angles of a triangle always add up to two right angles? The answer is that the action of putting together three lines to make a triangle has the inevitable consequence that the angles add up to two right angles.

There are undoubtedly some 'inner truths'. Usually these are 'organizing principles'.

It was the contribution of Socrates, Plato and Aristotle to take the truth that there might be some inner truths in certain instances and to extend this to all matters. This is a totally unjustified extrapolation and is simply a 'belief truth' itself. It is as much a religion as any other religion that depends on belief truth. The result is that clusterings of convenience come to be treated as 'true definitions' simply because no one around has the wit to refute them.

Induction may reveal 'inner truths' as in the grandmother example given above, where a number of instances can lead you to guess the principle being used. But in most cases induction is no more than a shorthand summary of past experience.

There is a very close relationship between 'truth', 'true definitions' (boxes, categories, etc.) and judgement. All three go tightly together to give us our traditional thinking system. The Socratic method really refers to the discovery or setting up of the 'true definitions', but in practice we can extend it to the judgement of whether something fits a definition, because this is partly how Socrates set up the definitions in the first place.

Hunting for game birds is taken very seriously in the English countryside. The novice who is taken shooting for the first time is hugely embarrassed to find that he has shot at a blackbird in the mistaken belief that it was a pheasant. The humiliation is extreme. Towards the end of the season the hunter is equally embarrassed at shooting down a high-flying hen pheasant when 'cocks only' has been ordained by the gamekeeper. So with time and effort the hunters become very skilled at recognizing each bird. If the recognition is exact then the action follows automatically. Is that a pheasant? Yes, it is a pheasant. Bang!

A doctor learns the disease 'boxes' in medical school. He or she learns how to look for symptoms by direct examination or through tests (X-rays, blood tests, etc.) and learns how to come to a conclusion or make a judgement. Once the judgement has been made then the treatment is quite easy, because it is more or less automatic or standardized.

So judgement and 'boxes' are the link between circumstance and appropriate action. If something is poisonous you do not eat it. If someone is dishonest you watch that person carefully. If a government is not democratic you condemn it.

So the thinking operation is:

1. Set up the boxes.
2. Regard them as 'true' or 'absolute'.
3. Judge something into a box.
4. Take the action indicated by the box.

The method simplifies life and seems to work. It has always been the basis of our education, the basis of our thinking, the basis of our behaviour.

Judgement is used to validate the definition and to reject the 'untrue', as discussed in a previous section. Judgement is then used in 'recognition' and to pop things into the established boxes. It is this last aspect of judgement which concerns me here.

I am not impressed by the argument that in its purest form the system works because 'inner truth' is restricted to a very few areas and because the 'boxes' are designed very carefully to take the system into account. I am sure that this is occasionally true. But we have to look at the practical aspect of the method, where people make category judgements and dangerous generalizations. The question is whether it is really feasible to hope that people can be thoroughly educated to use the system in its purest sense or whether the system itself is so open to poor use that we had better change the system. I can only say, from my experience, that some of those who claim to be the teachers of the best way to use the critical system are themselves every bit as guilty of its poor use as anyone else. This suggests that the system is at fault.

In most cases induction is no more than a shorthand summary of past experience.

One of the major limitations of the judgement system is that it is reactive rather than proactive. This means that you criticize ideas rather than create them. The generative capacity is very low. It is restricted to thesis/antithesis/synthesis, which is only a tiny fraction of the creative potential in any situation. I shall deal with this aspect in a later section; what concerns me here is the 'judgement' that puts things into the waiting boxes.

The waiting boxes are standard, fixed and stereotyped. This means that we see things in a somewhat rigid and fixed way. While this may make for convenience, it does not make for the most appropriate action. The element of exploration is very restricted. It is restricted to which boxes are relevant and which of these is to be used.

Complex situations are oversimplified and forced into standard boxes which simply ignore certain factors.

We are forced to look at the world with the perceptions, concepts and language which were set down in previous times. Our experience has been frozen, fixed and fossilized into existing boxes. Yet there is an absolute mathematical need to change these boxes. We cannot do this, because as soon as we step outside the established boxes then the traditionalists point out the error. So the traditional thinking method is excellent at defending and preserving its inadequacies – because it claims to have set the rules of the game: use these standard boxes.

People are forced to use the judgement/box system because education has not developed and has not taught the exploration/design system.

The classification habits of psychologists, especially in the USA, are a clear example of this traditional habit. Suppose you 'judge' people into different categories or boxes. What does that mean? Does it mean that you are not going to employ her because she is 'right-brain'? Does it mean that you do not put him into research because he is an 'adaptor' rather than an 'innovator'? Very quickly this becomes a dangerous form of intellectual racism. I am sure that the original developers of the tests used did not see them as discriminating devices and did not feel that 'action' should follow the judgement. I am sure they regarded them only as 'another factor' in carrying out an exploration of a person's capabilities. Even then I am not too happy, because such tests are based on 'what is' rather than 'what can be'. Should we test a person's thinking ability or should we design methods which will increase that ability considerably? I am much afraid that we are still too hung up on that 'inner-truth' belief which is more interested in what is there than in what can be put there.

In school we are always asking students to judge, to categorize, to analyse and to dissect. There is far less emphasis on exploration, possibility, generation, creativity and design. There is more emphasis on what things *are* than on what you can make things *be*. This false emphasis arises directly from the Socratic notion that knowledge is virtue. If you have knowledge then action is easy. We pay much attention to literacy and numeracy but not to 'operacy'. This is a word I invented many years ago to indicate the 'skills of action'. Design is a key aspect of operacy. 'How do we design a way forward?'

People are forced to use the judgement/box system because education has not developed and has not taught the exploration/design system.

20 POSSIBILITY VS. CERTAINTY

Most people believe that Western progress, in those areas where it has occurred, is due to our traditional thinking system with its search for the absolute truth; with its classifications and category judgements; with its arguments and refutations. I do not believe this to be so. The main driving force of Western progress has been the 'possibility' system. This is immensely powerful, and also essential. It is essential because of the way the brain works. As a patterning system, the brain can only 'see' what it is prepared to see. The analysis of information will not produce new ideas – merely a selection from existing standard ideas. It is the possibility system that creates a hypothesis.

Once we have a hypothesis then we can direct our search for further information, just as a detective with a hypothesis knows where to look. Once we have a hypothesis then we can set up special circumstances to test that hypothesis, as in an experiment. Once we have a hypothesis then we can organize our information, experience and perceptions according to that hypothesis. A hypothesis does not prove anything at all: it is merely an organizing framework.

Another part of the possibility system is 'vision', which allows us to imagine where we might be. We can then work towards that vision. All this is totally different from just analysis – judging and describing 'what is' at the moment.

The possibility system opens up creativity. You can try things out. You do not have to be 'right' at each step. You can change paradigms instead of having to be judged in the existing paradigm.

Technology in China was far advanced 2,000 years ago. China was well ahead of Western civilization. Then the progress came to an end. Once the scholars had got hold of things, everything was neatly labelled and described. Experimentation, provocation and possibility were not permitted in the 'academic' world. It seems that China never developed an appreciation of the value of the hypothesis.

In Western thinking, education and culture we greatly underestimate the power and importance of the 'possibility' system. We are uncomfortable with it precisely because it does not easily fit into the traditional thinking methods developed by the Gang of Three.

Remember that Plato, with his fascist tendencies, was reacting sharply to the chaotic world suggested by the sophists in which truth was relative, perception was paramount and there was an intellectual culture of 'anything goes'. The reaction to this chaos was to come down heavily on the side of absolute and unchangeable 'inner truth' or 'ideal forms'. Possibility was to be excluded in favour of certainty.

Courts of law, as we currently operate them, have to come to conclusions. Is the accused guilty or innocent? That is a sharp, hard-edged and absolute judgement. Mistakes do get made and the wrong people do get executed. But that is a price that has to be paid for operating a practical system. The key point is that the decision has to be made with certainty on the evidence available at that time.

Our traditional and usual logic system (Aristotelian in origin) cannot work if we remove the concepts of true/false and inclusion/exclusion. We cannot work the logic system on 'maybe', 'sometimes' or 'possibly'. This is because we think by moving sequentially from one 'true' or correct step to the next one. That is exactly why Socrates kept stopping to ask his listeners if they agreed. That gave him an accepted step from which to move forward to the next step. Sequential thinking demands certainty and absolutes. Parallel thinking, as we shall see later, does not.

A more constructive approach is to allow the contradictory views to exist in parallel and then to design a way forward.

If we say that swans may have long necks but may also have short necks then there is little point in putting a long neck into the definition of a swan. Once we learn that swans can indeed be black, then 'whiteness' is no longer a useful part of the definition of a swan. The judgement/box system of thinking is useless without certainty. We must keep saying 'all' and 'never', otherwise our boxes (or sets) have little practical action value.

Children in school are encouraged to be definite rather than tentative. It is a historical fact that the Treaty of Utrecht took place at a certain date. There is no room for 'possibility' in the fact of the date, though the student's certainty may not rise above 'possibility' levels. So in the world of description, classification and analysis there is little space for the importance of 'possibility'.

Sequential thinking demands certainty and absolutes. Parallel thinking, as we shall see later, does not.

Then there is the considerable, and genuine, fear that 'possibility' simply opens up the floodgates to all sorts of nonsense. If a child is asked how he or she might escape from a burning building, should the teacher accept the 'possibility' that Superman might swoop down and rescue the child? It is not too difficult to distinguish between realistic possibilities and fantasy possibilities. Children usually have a very good sense of the 'game' they are playing. Is it the game of reality or the game of fantasy?

A practical difficulty with the possibility system is that it is impossible to attach the traditional labels of true/false and right/wrong. They no longer have their sharp-edged convenience.

Most important of all, contradictions can exist in the world of possibilities. Implicitly, Western logic is based on the non-acceptance of contradictions. Many logical refutations consist in showing that the position held is 'contradictory'. If you have a definition of a 'chair' and you judge a piece of furniture, you decide whether it 'is' a chair or 'is not' a chair. The item cannot both 'be' and 'not be' a chair at the same time. This is at the very heart of the traditional thinking system. The use of 'possibility' destroys the contradiction process:

'Maybe it is a chair and maybe it is not a chair.'

'Maybe it is both a chair and not a chair at the same time.'

Traditional thinking cannot accept contradictions, because entry into the box or exclusion from the box will determine action and you cannot have action and non-action at the same time.

In the parallel-thinking system we can easily accept contradictions as 'parallel' statements which can coexist alongside each other. Attention then moves to 'what do we do next?' The emphasis is not on judgement but on the design of action.

Many conflicts exist because there is the belief that one party is right and the other party is wrong. It is felt that the conflict can never be resolved, because the parties want contradictory and mutually exclusive things. So we seek to exercise judgement. A more constructive approach is to allow the contradictory views to exist in parallel and then to design a way forward.

So pervasive are the Western habits of thinking that even in ordinary conversation we are inclined to say 'all' or 'never':

'All restaurants have menus.'

'Cats never swim.'

'All politicians are untrustworthy.'

'All men are brutes.'

'All women are deceitful.'

The result is that we are either mistaken or unable to make the statement if we do not want to be mistaken. Yet the value of the remark is just as high if we use different words:

'Most ...'

'By and large ...'

'Quite often ...'

'Some ...'

'There are ...'

It is possible to give an impression or to offer a summary of personal experience without having to enter the 'absolutes' system at all. This is the key difference between judgement and exploration. Judgement demands sharp-edged certainty. Exploration puts possibilities in parallel without having to judge them immediately.

21 EXPLORATION VS. JUDGEMENT

'*I think* that house is Georgian.'

'It cannot be Georgian – the windows are all wrong.'

'I also think it is Victorian.'

'It cannot be both Georgian and Victorian – those styles are completely opposite. Make up your mind.'

That short conversation illustrates the difference between exploration and judgement. The exploring person is putting forward possibilities. The judging person is using judgement in two distinct ways. The first way is to judge the suggestion immediately and to reject it – probably on good grounds. The second way is to insist that two more or less mutually exclusive styles cannot coexist: there has to be a choice between them.

There are two (at least) types of conversation. In the first type the other person challenges you at every point and will not let you get away with anything. Every point has to be argued and proved. In the second type the other person listens and does not interrupt. When you have come to a conclusion, the other person might then come back to a point you have made – a point on which the conclusion rests – and ask you to prove that point.

We are taught to use judgement as a 'gatekeeper'. This gate-keeper checks the credentials of everything that we allow into our minds. Everything has to be checked as true or false. It is like a modern office building with tight security at the entrance. The security has to be tight because once you have entered you are free to move around and no one bothers you any more. There is only the 'entry' check, so it has to be very good. That is how we have been taught to use judgement.

Consider the difference between a chain and a rope. With a chain each and every link has to be sound, otherwise the chain is useless and will break. With a rope, however, each strand does not have to be sound. Some can be weak and the other strands will take the strain. The rope is a 'parallel' system. The chain is a sequential system.

In exploration you allow in possibilites. They remain as possibilities. Even mutually exclusive possibilities are allowed to enter and are laid alongside each other. In the analogy of the building security, there would be no entrance check but every entrant would be regarded as a possible risk all the time he or she was in the building. There would be no one-step security clearance. There would be no gatekeeper function, and no permanent acceptance either. All 'possibilities' would be regarded with suspicion.

This security analogy makes another important point. With the gatekeeper use of judgement, once there has been clearance and something has been accepted as 'true' then that something is never re-examined. That is how Socrates could make his points. He got his listeners to accept one point after another. If the listeners had once said 'maybe' then the whole chain would have collapsed.

The gatekeeper use of judgement leads to two possible errors:

1. We permanently reject something that is actually correct – but perhaps within a different paradigm.
2. We permanently accept something which seems right at this moment in time – but not in other circumstances. It was to avoid this error that the sophists, and their equivalent today, preferred the relative notion of truth – except in 'game truth' (where we set up things).

With parallel thinking we enrich the field with 'possibilities' and then proceed to design the most appropriate action or decision.

A stinking fish can stink out the whole refrigerator. Similarly the acceptance of a false assumption can eventually wreck all the thinking based on it. In the gatekeeper system, once we have put the fish in the refrigerator then we forget all about it. In the parallel system, we keep everything out in the open and acknowledge that the fish may stink.

In the parallel system, we are not going to keep the fish around for any length of time.

The gatekeeper use of judgement can be an offensive weapon. The arguer sets up dichotomies – usually false – and then forces the listener to choose between them.

'This man is either honest or dishonest.'

'Either we go into Europe or we do not.'

'We give in to the union demands or we stand our ground.'

The listener is immediately given an either/or choice and tends to choose the most acceptable. The speaker then has the listener where he or she wants the listener. The next step proceeds. Socrates used this very method almost all the time. His listeners were constantly offered choices in which the 'reasonable' choice was much stronger than the 'unreasonable' one. In this way Socrates edged his listeners along.

It is usually difficult for a listener to say:

'I want both of those.'

'I don't accept those choices.'

'I see no need to make that choice at this point.'

In the traditional thinking system we see the very early use of judgement. This is characteristic of the system. This early use of judgement may serve either of two functions:

1. The gatekeeper function, to accept or reject what is offered.
2. The identifying function, to find the right 'box'.

In any classification system there is a great deal of attention at the edges. Does this go into box A or box B? Is this a fruit or a vegetable? Do I treat this as a personal expense or as a business expense? A great deal of education and a great deal of philosophy is focused on just such discriminations. This is absolutely essential in the judgement/box system. You have to be sure where you are putting things, because they will stay there.

In the parallel system you would be less concerned at the beginning. You would say: 'Let us treat it as both A and B.' You might make a copy and put one copy in file A and another in file B. When all the factors have been collected and it is time to make a decision or to take action, only then does a decision have to be made. It may be that part of the expense is a legitimate business expense and part is a personal expense.

We are used to classification 'boxes'. Something has to be in one box or another. This point is a 'plus' point or a 'minus' point. How can it be both? But it can – depending on the circumstance and the perspective. Instead of classification boxes which are based on the judgement system, we can have exploratory windows. You look out of window A and you see what you see. You look out of window B and you see what you see. There may be a lot of overlap. Someone may see through window A what you see through window B. It does not matter. What is seen does not belong to A or to B: you are interested in the total view. The windows are merely aids to getting a fuller view. So when students use the PMI attention-directing tool there is not the intention to classify observed points as 'plus', 'minus' or 'interesting': the intention is deliberately to look through these 'windows' and to see what you see. There may be overlap. The same point may be found under different headings.

It is all a matter of emphasis and of sequence. I am not 'against' judgement. Judgement is an important mental operation and is essential at some points. It is a matter of sequence. Do we judge first or do we explore first and then judge after we have explored and after we have designed the action or decision? The Socratic system was very concerned with judging right away possibly because it was intended to deal with subjects, like ethics, where this was somewhat more appropriate. The difference is suggested in Figure 6. As regards emphasis, we put far too much emphasis on judgement and far too little on exploration.

To suggest that we have to reject judgement in order to embrace exploration is to fall exactly into the trap set by the traditional thinking system, which insists that you must attack something in order to suggest something else. Judgement is fine in its right place. Judgement is very useful, but it is totally insufficient without exploration and generation of ideas.

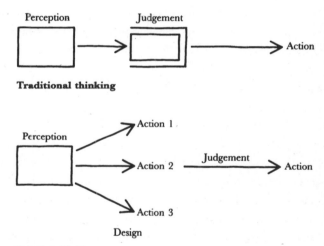

Figure 6   **Parallel thinking**

Then there is the matter of the 'outcome' of the judgement. Should this be the absolute certainty that we normally seek? Should things be put into their 'truth' boxes? Or should the outcome of judgement also be a 'possibility', but a rather stronger possibility than the exploration 'possibility'?

'I judge this to be true.'

'I judge this to be a strong possibility.'

Judgement does not have to imply the true/false dichotomy with which Plato and the Gang of Three endowed it in order to escape the relativism of the sophists.

As in the analogy of the chain, judgement insists that we have to be 'right' at each stage. In Figure 7 a motorist is proceeding along a narrow road. There is a turning to the left, but obviously it leads backwards and away from the direction in which the motorist is proceeding, so the motorist rejects it. Yet, with a helicopter view, we can see that the side road leads to a much better road that leads in the desired direction. Should the motorist have explored the side road?

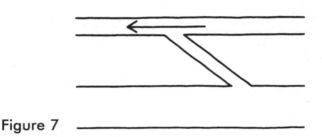

Figure 7

Probably not, because we have to use practical frames of judgement. The purpose of the illustration is to show that judgement is a matter of 'practicality', not truth. In 'truth' the side road was valuable. As a practical strategy the side road could not be taken. When driving along a motorway it is sometimes necessary to take a turning heading south when you really want to go north. In this known context we accept the need to go in an apparently opposite direction.

The provocative techniques used in the deliberate creativity of lateral thinking seek to set up instabilities in order to get us out of the comfortable ruts of our usual patterns which have been formed by a particular sequence of experience. There is the new word 'po' which I invented many years ago to signal a provocative operation. With provocation we are allowed to say things which we know to be incorrect in order to 'move forward' from the statement to a useful new idea. The asymmetric nature of patterns in human perception makes something of the sort essential.

We might say:

'Po cars have square wheels.'

'Po the factory is downstream of itself.'

Having to be correct at evey step makes creativity virtually impossible.

The first statement is totally contrary to our understanding of engineering principles. The second statement is contrary to normal logic: how can something be in two places at the same time? Judgement would have to throw out both statements as being total nonsense. Yet from the first statement through the process of 'movement' (a formal mental operation) we move on to the concept of 'intelligent suspension' in cars. Using 'movement' on the second provocation we move on to the idea that if a factory is built on the side of a river then the 'input' must be placed downstream of the 'output' so the factory is the first to get its own pollution – and needs to take steps to clean it up.

Having to be correct at every step makes creativity virtually impossible.

The instant judgement of an emerging idea will almost always lead to rejection of that idea. In the Six Hats system of exploration such rejection would not be permitted, because the 'black' hat would only come later. It is not my intention here to go into the details of the techniques of lateral thinking, which have now been in use for many years with considerable success.

Those who are interested in that aspect should read the books indicated below.*

Having looked at the gatekeeper aspect of judgement, which is concerned with true/false and accept/reject, we come now to the identification role of judgement: into which 'box' does this go?

I have a fax machine with a little window which indicates what is going on. When things are not going on, the window indicates 'Error 003'. I look this up and it says: 'No recording paper. Action: insert new recording paper.' Or it might be 'Error 127'. I look this up and it says: 'Facsimile terminal not compatible. Action: contact the other operator.' This is very sensible indeed. How else is the operator going to know what is going on and how to take the right action?

The fax machine has itself identified the error. Once the error has been identified then the action follows automatically from that identification.

The immediate use of judgement for box identification is exactly similar. We make the diagnosis. We make the judgement. Once we have judged that something fits into a particular box or category then the subsequent action is preset, easy and automatic.

There are general boxes like 'attractive', 'unpleasant', 'friend' and 'enemy', with some general actions attached to them: 'seek out', 'take further', 'avoid', 'be careful', etc.

In some cases animals react immediately, out of instinct, as soon as their senses have been given enough information to identify a situation. The box/judgement system seeks to do the same for humans – instant judgement to give identification and then instant action. Life is this way simplified.

---

* *Serious Creativity* (London: Vermilion, 2015). Also *Lateral Thinking: A Textbook of Creativity* (London: Penguin, 2009) and *Lateral Thinking for Management* (London: Penguin, 1990).

In a preceding section I have dealt with the rigidities and dangers of the box system and its certainty. It may be useful, however, to point out again that the action which follows from the box identification ('He is an enemy') is automatic and crude. There is very little 'design' of action. In fact the traditional thinking system believes that 'knowledge' is enough and that action is easy: you just move towards the good things and away from the bad ones. That is why we have paid so little attention to 'operacy'.

In contrast to the automaticity of the judgement/box method, with parallel thinking we enrich the field with 'possibilities' and then proceed to design the most appropriate action or decision. When we have the proposed course of action, or decision, then we relate this to our needs, to the available information, to the situation. This final stage is a sort of judgement or comparison process.

'He has no experience running a hospital. We should reject him.'

That would be the normal judgement approach.

'His experience is in banking and in running a large hotel.'

'He is good at getting things done.'

'He gets on well with people.'

'In a way a hospital is a sort of hotel.'

'He can make decisions.'

'The other applicants are very traditional.'

'Having considered all the factors I think we should try him out.'

The parallel exploration puts down many more factors. This is in contrast to the judgement approach, which seeks, as soon as possible, for a basis for acceptance/rejection.

There is a fundamental difference between parallel thinking and the judgement-dominated traditional thinking system. The latter arose directly from the concern for 'truth' which was so important to Plato and subsequently to the Church and to feudal societies.

It should also be remembered that the original purpose of education was that a small band of people in society (lawyers, scribes, thinkers) should 'know' things. Such people would be called upon for their input when the people of action (kings, builders, merchants) needed a knowledge input. This is very similar to a person today using a computer database to obtain information as required. So it is not at all surprising that education has never been concerned with action, with design or with creativity. Our admiration for a 'classical education' fossilizes that attitude. Knowing has always been more important for education than exploring. So judgement has been taught as the dominant feature in thinking.

22 DESIGN VS. ANALYSIS

I have often suggested that Western civilization would have been some 300 years ahead of where it is at the moment if it had not been saddled with our traditional thinking system. The obvious retort to that suggestion is to ask why those civilizations which were not saddled with the same thinking system are not far ahead instead of being, apparently, behind. There are two possible replies to that. One is that these other civilizations also had their inhibitors. In India it was the 'acceptance' of the world and adjustment to it as illustrated in the caste system. In China it was the dominance of the scholars and the lack of the hypothesis. In Africa it may have been contentment with a stable society which put human values above technical progress.

Where the West has made progress, as in technical matters, I believe this to be due to the 'possibility' system, which is different from the 'truth' system (though this gave the motivation for search). I also believe that the cooler North was more action-oriented than the warmer South.

An example of what happens when there is a culture shift away from stability towards change is to be found in Japan and the astonishing rate of progress following the Meiji restoration in 1868. The very rapid rate of industrial development in Korea (a fortyfold increase in GDP since 1960) also indicates what can happen.

The technical side of Western thinking has never been mainstream. It has carried on in spite of persecution and neglect. The scientist Roger Bacon was locked up for the last 15 years of his life on the magnificent charge of 'uttering novelties'. This happened in medieval Europe, but not in some primitive backwater: it happened in the intellectual centre of Oxford.

Western thinking has been obsessed with 'what is' rather than with 'what can be'. Western thinking has been obsessed with 'analysis' rather than with 'design'. This is hardly surprising given the origin of that thinking in the Gang of Three.

Socrates was concerned with 'the search for the truth'. You do not design the truth, you find it. Socrates believed that virtue is knowledge and that wrongdoing is only due to ignorance. So if you lay bare the truth people will behave virtuously. Promoting virtue is not a matter of creating pragmatic rules but of finding the 'truth'. He sought to tease out the truth by using induction. From an examination of multiple examples he hoped to extract the 'true definition'. As I have mentioned, this is somewhat different from the group of grammarians trying to tease out the rules of grammar. At some point they would have had to 'design' rules based on what they had found. Socrates was not prepared to use any element of design – or at least Plato would not let him do so.

Analysis is a very worthwhile operation. Analysis takes a complex situation and seeks to tease out what is going on. What factors are involved? What are the interactions? What are the elements? This allows us to understand complex things. It allows us to start to understand new things. It allows us to predict behaviour. It allows us to seek to control events. Analysis takes a situation and seeks to break it down into parts which we can recognize and which therefore link in to our existing knowledge boxes. Is there anything wrong with this? Not at all. It is a most useful part of thinking. But there are considerations to be considered:

1. We have become obsessed with analysis and spend far too much time on analysis and far too little on design.
2. The holistic interactions of a complex system may be lost when it is broken down into elements.
3. Analysis provides one way of looking at a situation and may seek to preclude other ways of analysing the same situation
4. Analysis claims to have discovered the 'true' situation.
5. Analysis can provide spurious elements which then acquire a life of their own in new 'dances' of intellectual effort.

Quite obviously education sees its role as describing 'what is'. Universities are the worst, with an almost total obsession with analysis. This is not surprising. Builders get on with building and describers get on with describing. But the describers have as their work the control of education and of culture. So analysis and description become the dominant intellectual idioms. Anyone who goes through school education and university comes out the other end believing that analysis and description are enough. They may be enough to deal with 'what is', but they are totally inadequate in dealing with 'what may be'. So all these excellent minds are wasted – trapped in the limited world of analysis.

Take an ordinary bottle of mineral water. There is the cap. Then there is the opening which the cap occludes. Then there is the neck of the bottle. Then the body of the bottle that holds the label. Then there is the bottom which allows the bottle to stand upright. Now between the neck and the body there is the shoulder. Should there also not be an 'intermediate zone' which links the body to the bottom? Then what about the intermediate zone which links the opening to the neck? And the 'sub-shoulder' zone which is just under the shoulder? There is no limit to analysis once we start to enjoy the game.

Western civilization has been thoroughly brainwashed into believing that 'truth' is enough.

So much of philosophy and psychology has been of this 'games with analysis' nature. Is such activity incorrect? No more than a very elaborate analysis of the mineral water bottle is incorrect. Is it necessary? Probably not. Is it useful? Probably not.

I have already mentioned the obsession in psychology with measurement and grouping. We want to know 'what is'. There is much less emphasis on designing methods of change in order to explore 'what can be'. The defenders of the 'what is' measurements will claim that they need to assess 'what is' in order to have a base for designing 'what can be'. In that case there should be an equal emphasis on 'what can be' in terms of grants, publications, etc. There is not.

Western civilization has been thoroughly brainwashed into believing that 'truth' is enough. But truth does not grow crops, design irrigation systems or create new ideas. All that requires design.

There is a difference between measuring, describing or photographing a house and designing and building that same house. We might claim that knowledge of 'what is' also includes knowledge of 'what is the right way to build a house'. But if this was fixed in the past then all houses would be the same. We need to develop the thinking skills of design, not just put out a permanent, unchanging handbook of housebuilding.

Socrates believed that 'truth', 'justice', 'morality', etc. were unchanging. We believe that to this day. Why? Because we believe they are like Pythagoras's theorem about triangles, which will not change (as long as we stay with a flat surface).

Designing means bringing into being something which was not there before. This could be repetition of something which already exists. It could be a random creation – like a mess.

In between these two extremes there is a need to 'design' the new thing to meet some end which might be practical or aesthetic or just pleasurable.

We have become obsessed with analysis and spend far too much time on analysis and far too little on design.

You could set out to design a meal, a party, a piece of pottery, a building, a park, music, a better legal system, a better democratic system, a new form of corporate entity or a new concept of employment.

We permit design in the 'art world' and in certain specialized professions, but it is not part of general education. Contrast Italy, which trains some 40,000 architects a year but only needs 2,000, with the USA, where for 'architect' (relatively speaking) you should read 'lawyer'. The most popular faculty in the USA is law. The design habits of being trained in architecture enable Italy to remain at the forefront of style in almost every area. The lawyer habits lead to a litigious society.

Quite apart from specialized professions, everyone needs to learn the skills of design. The skills of judgement are inadequate. We need to design alternatives for action. We need to design alternative ways of looking at things. We need to design decisions. We need to design ways out of conflicts and negotiations.

Why have we come to believe that the 'search' idiom is enough? Why have we so neglected to develop the 'design' idiom? The answer is simple: the Gang of Three who formed Western thinking habits were concerned with search (though Aristotle was more practical than the others).

We badly need to design new words. Otherwise we remain trapped in the baggage of existing words and unable to use new perceptions. I designed the term 'lateral thinking', which has now become part of the language. I designed the word 'po' to indicate a provocation. This is an even more powerful term because it permits us to do something which is otherwise not allowed in language – to make and to signal a provocation. The use of this is more restricted. I believe the term 'parallel thinking' will catch on and become widely used. There is also a new word 'popic', which I shall describe in a later section. Such words seem gimmicky and unnecessary until you become familiar with what they enable you to do.

Design is essential for parallel thinking. With traditional thinking it is enough to identify the situation and then the action is indicated. With traditional thinking it is enough to be right at each step and some sort of action will follow. With parallel thinking we enrich the field with possibilities which are laid alongside each other. The next step is to design the way forward.

In a previous section I indicated that traditional problem-solving depended on analysis to identify the cause of the problem followed by removal of this cause. This works well where it works. But there are problems where the cause cannot be found or, if found, cannot be removed. There, again, it is necessary to design a way forward. Further analysis will not help.

What are the principles and methods of design? How do we do it? It is not the purpose of this book to offer a design manual. That is a whole area in itself, and there are different approaches. But we can look here at a few of the principles:

1. Sometimes just laying out the factors and desires in parallel can give so clear a picture that the choice of action is made clear.

2. There can be a genuine attempt to reconcile contradictions by treating them as provocations and using 'movement' to go forward to a practical idea.

3. There can be value in using deliberate creativity to open up new starting-points and to change existing concepts.

4. A direct focus on creating value. The need to identify and extract the apparently required values and then to find a way to deliver them.

5. Moving to an 'ideal' design and then working backwards from that.

6. Allowing the possibilities to 'self-organize' into an outcome.

7. Using specific techniques like the 'flowscape'* to find out how perceptions interact and to find the sensitive points for action.

8. The traditional method of working systematically to satisfy the needs and constraints.

9. Using the big-jump method to open up a new concept (perhaps using lateral thinking) and then seeking to modify this to make it practical and acceptable.

10. Designing for the top priorities and then fitting the lesser priorities into the design.

11. Borrowing standard approaches and adapting them if necessary.

12. Setting up a trial-and-error process in which a course of action will gradually become moulded into a better one.

13. Setting up a practical test system so that many alternatives can be tested (computer simulations, etc.).

14. Using techniques like the 'concept fan'.†

15. Seeking to challenge the starting-point, boundaries, assumptions, objectives, etc.

As useful as these methods might be, the basic attitude of 'design' is even more important. In correcting students' examination papers, I have often been struck by how competent students are at analysis and how poor at the design of action. That is not surprising, since they have had so little education in design. Even in medical school the whole emphasis is on

---

* See my book *Water Logic* (London: Penguin, 1994).

† See my book *Serious Creativity*.

diagnosis. Very little time is spent on the design of treatment. This is not because treatment is always changing and will become obsolete when the student has qualified (which is true enough) but because there is an underlying belief that diagnosis is enough and that treatment is automatic and easy. In the future this will all change. We shall find that there is no such thing as a standard treatment but that different patient profiles will require differently designed treatments. Even then there will be different phases of treatment. Treatment is a strategy, not an automatic response to a 'box'-type diagnosis.

Without design we can only deal with standard situations in standard ways. Analysis is an attempt to turn new situations into the standard situations with which we can deal. That is why, on the whole, we are so very ineffective in dealing with new situations – like the conflicts that arose after the collapse of the Soviet Union.

23 INFORMATION VS. IDEAS

Thinking is no substitute for information. Information is essential. Information has a high value. Information is a 'good thing'.

Since information is good, more information is even better. There are people who believe that if you get enough information then the information will do your thinking for you. Many people in business believe that. Of course, if information really could make the decisions then we should not need people, because information in a computer would flow along to give the decision output. This may happen in the future. For the moment, the human being is a sort of junction who adds to the information, ideas, values and politics and then passes on to a decision.

In the past, information was the real bottleneck, so any improvement in information would lead to an improvement in thinking and in the quality of decisions. Information access and handling (by computers) have widened that bottleneck. So we move on to the next bottleneck. This is 'thinking'. What do we do with the information? Most people in business and government have not fully faced that change.

If information is good, more information is better. This follows directly from the traditional thinking system. In a different book* I have dealt with the problem of the 'salt curve'.

* *I am Right, You are Wrong* (London: Penguin, 2009).

Food with no salt tastes bad; some salt tastes good; too much salt tastes bad. I indicated that traditional thinking has a very hard time with such situations. In a previous section I mentioned how Socrates had trouble with the definition of bravery. No knowledge meant that you were not brave, some knowledge meant you were brave, more knowledge might mean that you were not brave – and so on.

There are times when too much information clutters up the system, obscures what is really important, and reduces flexibility. If you have to go into the most minute details of every person you interview then the process is going to take so long that you are only able to interview a few people.

We love information because it is unquestionably valuable and it is easy to deal with – especially today.

Education loves information. There was a time when it was possible for education to give a student virtually all the known scientific knowledge. The attitude of accumulating all possible information has persisted even though it is, today, total nonsense to try to do so.

There is, however, a dilemma. Everyone knows that a little bit more of information is very valuable. So where do we draw the line and say that it is not practical to teach more information? Where do we draw the line in order to say that we should spend time on teaching thinking skills rather than on teaching more information? It is not at all easy – which is why it is not happening.

It is the concept through which we perceive the information that gives it any value.

Information is easy to handle. There are books and libraries. You can put a book before a student and keep the student busy that way. The sheer mechanics of information are practical and attractive.

Ideas are a different matter. How do we produce ideas on demand? We can read about other people's ideas, but that is information. We may believe that ideas are a sort of divine inspiration over which we have no control. That is an old-fashioned view. We can design and produce ideas as easily as we can produce information or even more easily. The deliberate and formal techniques of lateral thinking can do this and are currently being taught in some schools and colleges. There is no mystery about the processes.

Many people still believe that analysis of information will, itself, create new ideas. This is not so, since the brain can only see what it is prepared to see. The analysis of information will allow us to select an idea from our repertoire of standard ideas but not to find a new idea. To 'see' a new idea we have first to imagine or speculate, so that the idea has a brief existence in our mind. Then we may be able to see the idea in the information.

This is why hypothesis and 'possibility' have played so dominant a role in scientific development. Even today, people teach science as if it is all about collecting data and doing experiments. Yet the key driving force of science is the ability to create hypotheses. In practice it is very rare in any science course for students to be given training in creativity and in the generation of hypotheses. Designing experiments and analysing data are an important part of science, but the hypothesis comes first. Nor is it always enough to have simplistic hypotheses like the hypothesis that X affects Y in some way. A correlation might be shown, but real progress comes about only when some model can be conceived. A stack of correlations is not worth much. Yet most of science today is done on that basis. The real work lies in imagining and testing mechanisms and models.

The analysis of information will allow us to select an idea from our repertoire of standard ideas but not to find a new idea.

Analysis of the sales of life insurance might suggest that single people are not heavy buyers. Why should they be? They have no families that might be affected by their sudden death. So the insurance company sees no market in single people. The analysis of information has shown 'what is' in the usual way. But if the concept of life insurance is changed to include the 'living-needs benefits' concept devised by Ron Barbaro in Canada (using lateral thinking) then, suddenly, life insurance is very attractive to single people because it also becomes catastrophic-illness insurance. The new concept is that if the insured person gets a serious illness which might be fatal then the insurance company will immediately pay out 75 per cent of the benefits which would otherwise be payable only on death. This money can be used for medical care.

The mathematical analysis of queues has been well worked out in operations research. It is possible to work out the waiting time, the number of serving positions needed, etc. But analysis of this sort is not going to lead to the new idea of having an extra serving position indicating that if you want to be served at that position then you pay a small fee. If too many people use that position the fee is raised. The money collected goes to open a further serving position, so benefiting everyone else as well. In this way someone in a hurry can set a value on his or her waiting time.

Ideas are organizing structures which put values and information together in new ways. Ideas need creative effort. Just collecting more information or analysing it more thoroughly will not produce ideas. This seems so obvious, and yet the bulk of our activity is spent on those activities and not on the generation of ideas. It could be that we do not see the value of ideas. This is hard to believe. It could be that we hope that analysis and more information will produce the needed ideas. Both experience and a simple understanding of the nature of self-organizing information systems will tell us that this is unlikely to be sufficient. We may believe that only chance and genius can produce ideas and there is nothing we can do about it. I suspect that this last belief is responsible for our lack of attention to serious creativity.

In all fairness, it has to be said that many of the approaches to creativity are so 'inspirational' and insubstantial that the field has something of a bad name. The belief that it is enough just to be liberated and to mess around with brainstorming does not build confidence in serious creativity. Yet those who want to investigate the field more thoroughly have an ample opportunity to do so. *

As in so many points in this book, it is not an either/or matter of either information or ideas. Both are needed. But, as with so many of the points I have sought to make about our traditional thinking system, we have been obsessed with just one aspect that is valuable but insufficient. This was the case with criticism, with judgement, with analysis and now with information.

Socrates was not obsessed with the search for information, although he did work by collecting as many examples as he could of what he sought to define. Our obsession with information arises more directly from the 'search-for-the-truth' idiom. We believe that information is 'truth' and therefore the more information we have the nearer we come to that 'full truth' which will tell us what to do.

We forget the very close relationship between ideas and information. It is the hypothesis idea which directs our search for information. It is the perceptual truth which helps us to interpret the information and give it credibility. It is the concept through which we perceive the information that gives it any value.

* See my book *Serious Creativity*.

There is a further point which needs mentioning. Universities only really got going at about the time of the Renaissance, although many had existed before. It was the Renaissance that opened up universities to new and secular thinking. Before that they had been largely concerned with theology and scripture. At the Renaissance it was obvious to everyone that the best ideas were going to be obtained by looking backwards at what had been done by the Greek thinkers and the Roman doers. So it was a unique period in history when looking backwards was indeed more progressive than looking forwards. This practice has continued to this day and is dignified by the name of 'scholarship'. Work is valued mainly in terms of how competently it looks backwards and rarely on how well it might affect the future. We esteem the value of collection more than we esteem the value of concepts. The nonsense of this will be shown in the future when computer programs will be able to look through the literature, pick out all relevant papers, and then extract from them (through theme search) all relevant paragraphs and put these together as a scholarly work. The library function which is the basis of so much university work will then be taken over by computers. People should then be freed to think.

24 MOVEMENT VS. JUDGEMENT

Judgement is a well-recognized thinking operation. 'Movement' is a different mental operation that is used from time to time but is rarely recognized as a deliberate and useful thinking operation.

Judgement is concerned with 'what is'. Judgement compares a situation or a suggestion to past experience and gives a verdict of 'match' or 'mismatch': this fits or this does not fit. Judgement is static.

Movement is concerned with 'what can be' or 'what may be'. Movement opens up possibilities. Movement looks at where the situation or suggestion leads. What follows next?

The judgement system is what I call 'rock logic',* because rock is static and has permanence.

The movement system is what I call 'water logic', because water is concerned with flow.

The key word in the judgement system becomes 'is'. The words 'yes' and 'no', 'true' and 'false', are really convenience versions of 'is'.

The key word in the movement system becomes 'to'. 'Where does this lead to?'

---

* See my book *Water Logic*.

Movement

Judgement

Judgement is concerned with establishing the solidity of each step in terms of past experience. Movement races ahead to open up possibilities that can come together as a new idea.

Judgement is about description. Movement is about creation.

We can say that sugar is white (or brown), but can we say that sugar is sweet? What we are really saying is that if we put the substance in our mouth it would give us the sensation of sweetness. So, in a sense, sugar 'leads to' the sensation of sweetness. Only sight and smell give instant appreciation; other qualities involve a 'test situation'. If you say that a suitcase is heavy, this is because you have lifted it already or you think that if you tried to lift it the case would be heavy.

You can say that shoes are black, or seem big, or are smelly. But if you say that shoes are comfortable or expensive then you are putting the shoes into a special situation: wearing them or buying them.

These special situations or test situations occur in our mind. It is in the inner world of perception that we run our thought experiments, which may look forward into the future or backwards into the past.

It is in the inner world of perception that the operation of 'movement' becomes important. Quite often in the outer world of reality one thing may lead to another. An insult may lead to a fight. A puncture will lead to stopping the car. A prize may lead to joy. But in the inner world of the patterns of perception one thing almost always leads to another.

It is in the inner world of perception that we run our thought experiments, which may look forward into the future or backwards into the past.

Imagine a knife lying on a table. Half an hour later that same knife is still lying on the table. Nothing has happened. But in the world of perception as soon as you see the knife several possible 'movements' occur. You may wonder how it got there. If it is a domestic type of knife you may think of food. If it is an ugly knife you may think of violence. The inner world of your mind moves on from the knife to something.

This movement may be passive, as in association, significance and meaning. What we see triggers a train of associations. What I am concerned with here is the 'active' use of movement as a deliberate mental operation. Judgement can be instant and automatic or it can be deliberate. The same applies to movement.

We use movement as a deliberate operation to open up possibilities for the exploration and creativity of parallel thinking:

'What follows?'

'What does this lead to?'

'What does this open up?'

'What are the possibilities?'

'Where do we go from here?'

'Movement' is a very valuable operation in creative thinking. With the provocative techniques of lateral thinking, movement is essential. In provocation we use the signal word 'po' to indicate a provocation, which is a statement we make purely for its 'forward effect' (to see what happens next).

In seeking to generate some new concepts for restaurants, we might put forward the provocation, 'Po a restaurant without food.'

Judgement would immediately reject that idea on at least two grounds:

1. There would be no reason for anyone to go.
2. Without food it would not be a restaurant at all.

Judgement might also add that even if people did go how would you get any payment from them?

It would be the correct role of judgement to relate this suggestion to our current experience.

It is not enough to judge. You cannot grow a garden just by wielding the shears. You do have to plant things from time to time.

Many traditional approaches to creativity, like brainstorming, would therefore insist on 'suspension' of judgement in order to avoid this instant rejection. But that is very weak. Suspending judgement is not itself an operation. What we need is the active mental operation of 'movement'.

If the restaurant does not provide food then that 'leads us on' to the idea that the customers bring their own food. This leads us on to the idea that the restaurant is a conveniently placed, well-decorated, indoor picnic place. Just as people might picnic on a riverbank in summer, so in winter they come to 'picnic' in the restaurant. The restaurant charges them for admission and service. The restaurant might provide the plates, etc., and possibly the drinks.

We can 'move' further. Where are the people going to get the food from? Perhaps they could buy the food from a whole range of takeaway vendors outside. This would now resemble the hawker restaurants in Singapore. Or they might buy frozen food from a nearby supermarket and each table in the restaurant would be equipped with a microwave oven.

There are various frames of 'movement' which go beyond simply association. One frame is to seek to extract a 'principle' or 'concept' and then to work forward with this.

'Po the restaurant has rude waiters.' The extracted principle is that the waiters have a definite personality and are not polite and invisible. From this we move forward to the waiters/waitresses being actors who perform a defined role. This role is described on the menu, and you can order your waiter/waitress just as you order a dish. You might choose a quarrelsome waiter in order to impress your guests with your macho style. You might choose a comedienne waitress for amusement. You might choose an eccentric waiter for the pleasure of surprise.

Another frame for 'movement' is to imagine the provocation being put into effect and watching what happens 'moment to moment' in order to move on to a new idea.

'Po the restaurant has no plates.' We could simply move on to the idea of eating off scrubbed wooden surfaces or banana leaves. This is not particularly interesting. We could imagine someone going to a restaurant that was known to have no plates. So the customer brings the plates. Now you would not want to be carrying plates around all the time, so you leave your plates in the restaurant and dine off them when you go to that restaurant. From that we 'move' on to a restaurant for business entertaining. A company has its plates embossed with its logo and special design. These plates are stored in the restaurant. Business entertaining takes place on your own plates. From the restaurant's point of view this also means that you would tend to do all your entertaining in that restaurant.

There are other frames for 'movement' such as: focus on the difference, special circumstances, positive aspects, etc. These are covered in specific books on the techniques of lateral thinking.*

In 'movement' we are really saying to ourselves: 'In this frame, where do we move to from this starting-point?'

There does not have to be a specified frame, and some people become very good at movement without needing to specify a frame. But movement is much more than just casual association.

While skill in movement is essential in lateral thinking and very valuable in any sort of creativity, it is also of a more general value.

The purpose of movement is to suggest things and to open up possibilities. This is all part of the exploratory process of parallel thinking. The possibilities generated exist in their own right in parallel. Not all are valuable. Not all are feasible. Not all are probable. Those that are not valuable, not feasible and not interesting will contribute little to the design of the final outcome. A buffet table can hold a wide variety of food. You put together your meal from a selection of the items. In the same way the final design of the outcome in parallel thinking is under no obligation to use or attend to all the possibilities that have been generated. You see the landscape and you choose your route.

* See page 126 for details of books dealing with lateral thinking.

Traditional thinking places the emphasis on judgement and the need to be right at every step. With creativity, you do not need to be right at every step so long as the final idea has value. We do not need to derive the value of the final idea from the validity of each step on the way there. We can assess the final idea in its own right. What does it offer? What are the risks? What are the costs? On the way to the final idea we may use provocations which we know to be 'wrong', but these act as stepping stones not judgement points. With the mental operation of movement we go forward from such points.

Movement has a generating function. It is not enough to judge. You cannot grow a garden just by wielding the shears. You do have to plant things from time to time.

It is a fundamental weakness of the traditional thinking system that it is so poor at generating. The attempted synthesis of thesis and antithesis is a very weak generating technique, both because its application is limited and because the process is not creative.

25 CREATE VS. DISCOVER

It is not fair to criticize a ballerina for not being an opera singer or a computer programmer. It is not fair to criticize the Socratic method for not being creative. Socrates and the other two members of the Gang of Three did not set out to be creative. They set out to discover the 'truth'. They were tired of the sophists who preferred to 'create' the truth with clever arguments and wordplay.

Discovery does bring into being new and important effects and understanding, as in science. The application of these discovered principles in technology creates value. Sometimes this application is so straightforward that we come to believe that the discovery element is all that matters and that application is easy. That is why we are more inclined to teach science than to teach technology in schools.

Do we discover laws or do we create them? We might discover certain principles, but the process of putting these principles into law requires the creativity of design. In some countries this is done with codified law, in others we rely on case law to mould the application of the law over time. The interpretation of the law by a succession of judges determines the law. This is evolution rather than creation, although each judge may need to be creative in giving a specific interpretation.

Do you discover dances or do you create them? You might discover some traditional folk dances, but you can also choreograph new dances. Do you discover new dishes or do you create them? Again, both approaches can contribute.

Do you have to be creative to create? The answer depends on our understanding of the word 'create'. If by 'create' we mean 'bring into being something which did not exist before', then you do not have to be 'creative'. It is enough to be constructive. The concept of 'design', which is very much part of parallel thinking and which I have mentioned extensively in previous sections, does not depend on 'creativity'. If you put together known things in such a way as to achieve an objective then neither the known things nor the way they are put together need be new.

Creativity involves change. This may be a change in concept, a change in perception or a change in the way of doing things.

You may design a house very competently. You may design a house which applies your own architectural style to this particular house. You may create new ways of using space which are new to you as well.

There is an overlap between being constructive, designing and being creative.

Creativity involves a willingness to challenge, a willingness to take risks, a willingness to be provocative and a willingness to step outside the judgements that are a summary of past experience. Traditionally, we have expected these characteristics to arise from the nature of certain personalities. You had to be a risk-taker to even think of an unusual idea. Today that is all changing. As we begin to understand creativity as pattern-switching in a self-organizing information system, we can develop certain processes which will greatly increase the flow of new ideas. A sober conformist can now, if he or she wishes, set up provocations and use them without having to feel eccentric or rebellious.

This does not mean that everyone is going to be equally creative. We can all learn the basic processes of mathematics, but some people are going to be much better mathematicians than others and some are even going to be mathematical geniuses.

Nevertheless, we see value in teaching mathematics to everyone. In exactly the same way we can teach creative thinking to everyone as part of their thinking equipment.

Will the fact that we can now teach creative thinking in a practical way make a difference to education? I doubt it. I think education is still very firmly bogged down in the traditional thinking idiom that insists that 'discovery' is all.

Creativity involves a willingness to challenge, a willingness to take risks, a willingness to be provocative and a willingness to step outside the judgements that are a summary of past experience.

The students 'discover the truth' by listening to teachers and reading books. Very occasionally there is the discovery of experimentation as well.

There is somehow a fear that if students develop creativity then they will not do things 'as they should'. There is a fear that things will get out of control. There is a fear that truth will become personal and optional, as some sophists suggested. Mostly, these fears arise from a misunderstanding of what creative thinking is about. Such misunderstanding believes that creativity is messing around, breaking all rules and being inspirational. Today we can look at serious creativity.

Although individual creativity occurs quite often in Western civilization we have never harnessed the potential creativity of people, because our traditional thinking system insists that discovery is enough.

We fully acknowledge that many of our ways of looking at the world are artificial constructs which have evolved over time.

We no longer believe in the 'divine right of kings' but see monarchy as a created type of politico-social position.

The interesting thing is that we do not have enough confidence to set out to create new concepts. We wait for them to evolve over time and then we 'discover' them as truths. Was Socrates really discovering an 'innate form' of justice which is present in people? Or was he discovering a common usage for the term 'justice' which had evolved over time? We would probably think that distinction irrelevant. The main thing is that he was 'discovering' something rather than creating it.

Although individual creativity occurs quite often in Western civilization we have never harnessed the potential creativity of people, because our traditional thinking system insists that discovery is enough. So creativity is limited to the arts, when it is needed everywhere else as well.

26 INNER WORLD VS. OUTER WORLD

The inner world is the world that exists in our minds: the world of perception. The outer world is the world out there: the reality with which we usually need to cope. The inner world is the train that you think leaves at 17.30. The outer world is the train you have missed because it actually left at 17.00.

Plato and Socrates were not directly concerned about people catching trains but indirectly they were much concerned. Obviously, if people have their own ideas about when trains run then everyone is going to be in a bit of a mess and society is not going to run smoothly. Would it not be better to have objective, printed timetables which people could consult and so get to the station on time? Does this merit being accused of fascism? Mussolini's greatest contribution to Italian culture was that he made the trains run on time.

Protagoras, the great sophist, was some 15 years older than Socrates and he and his fellow sophists taught/preached an extreme form of subjectivism. What seems to be the truth for me is the only truth for me – there can be no other. No man can tell another man that his perceptual truth is mistaken. Things are as you perceive them. Protagoras pointed out that all perceptions and judgements were equally true but not all were equally valid. If everyone perceives that a stream is not contaminated then that is the 'truth' for them, but this judgement is not valid because many of those drinking from the stream get cholera.

In an earlier book of mine I wrote about 'logic bubbles'.* A logic bubble is that temporary collection of perceptions, needs and emotions within which everyone acts perfectly logically. It is no use attacking the logic of people's actions, because to them they are indeed logical. The best you can do is to broaden or clarify their perceptions.

That is why teaching perceptual thinking (as in the *CoRT Thinking Lessons*†) can be so important.

Plato and Socrates claimed, believed and insisted that there was an objective truth out there somewhere. This was a truth which would be equally true for everyone. It would be strong enough to resist the efforts of the sophists to persuade people of other versions of the truth. There was the fundamental notion that the inner, subjective, world is inaccurate, misleading and capable of being deceived. We should seek to get rid of this dangerous inner world by bringing in the truths from the outer world so our inner view coincides as accurately as possible with the external world. Science should replace myth. Measurement should replace guessing. This is the idiom that has persisted to this day: a great suspicion of the unreliability of the inner world.

Because of this suspicion, we have paid virtually no attention to the very important matter of perception but have left that to the arts. We have concentrated instead on 'processing' which can be checked out in the outer world. You can measure triangles: you do not just have to imagine them.

Why use any map except the most accurate? Should not the inner world reflect as accurately as possible the outer world? Surely this is what discovery and education are all about?

* See my book *Future Positive* (London: Penguin, 1990).
† See page 84.

At one extreme there is an inner-world map which is so accurate a representation of the outer world that predictions can be made and useful action can be taken. At the other extreme the inner-world map is so very bizarre that the person is a danger to himself or herself and to those around. There are times when schizophrenics have an inner world which interprets the outer world in a totally unusual way. If we look at these two extremes then we are likely to favour the accurate inner-world map, because it permits us to operate effectively in the outer world where we earn a living and associate with people.

But the inner world has its own huge importance: love, dreams, beauty, fantasy, values, beliefs, etc. In the end it is the inner world which makes life worth living. The real purpose of the outer world is to keep us alive and to feed the dreams of the inner world.

Important as these values of the inner world might be, I am not concerned with them in this book. I am concerned with the 'thinking' value of the inner world. What does the inner world contribute to our thinking? Is the search for outer-world truth enough?

Possibilities exist in the inner world. Three people see a dog. One person, who is scared of dogs, thinks there is a possibility that the dog might attack. The second person thinks that the dog will attack only if the dog's territory is invaded. The third person, who likes dogs, thinks there is a possibility that the dog could be friendly if given the chance. Just as memories go backwards in our minds, so possibilities go forward in our minds. There may be evidence for a possibility but not yet any firm proof. Should we be allowed to hold that possibility because it exists in our inner mind? With parallel thinking there is no question: the possibility is valuable. With traditional thinking we should immediately proceed to judge it as soon as it appears.

In the end it is the inner world which makes life worth living. The real purpose of the outer world is to keep us alive and to feed the dreams of the inner world.

A hypothesis is an organizing possibility. In a previous section I commented upon the huge value of the hypothesis in Western technical progress. The hypothesis allows us to direct attention and to set up experiments. The hypothesis provides an organizing framework for what we see. The hypothesis gives us something to work towards and to work upon. The hypothesis is what we bring to the situation. The hypothesis exists only in the inner world.

Visions and objectives exist only in the inner world. An objective is something we want to work towards. We have to imagine the destination in order to plan our route. With a vision, we imagine the completed picture and this motivates us, and others, to set about making the picture reality. Without vision we should just react moment to moment, following the sensations and needs of the moment.

Concepts exist only in the mind. In Figure 8, if you choose to group A, P and K that is because you have some internal reason for doing so. The external grouping would have been A, B and C, because they are close to each other.

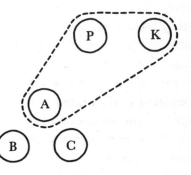

Figure 8

Concepts such as morality, justice and beauty exist only in our minds. Plato knew this full well, and yet he wanted to give them the unchanging objectivity of matters that exist in the objective world. So he created the notion of 'ideal forms' which have always existed in the mind but are true, universal and unchanging. So Plato acknowledged the huge importance of the inner world of perception but wanted to escape from its subjectivity and variability.

Belief is the most powerful of the inner-world behaviours. Belief goes beyond a tentative possibility to an inner-world 'truth'. In ordinary language, belief is sometimes used as being 'less than sure'. I prefer to call this a 'possibility'. I shall use the word 'belief' for something which is held 'to be so'. Belief is inner-world truth. You can believe that falling from a fourth-floor window will cause your death even if you have never tried it. You can believe that a stream contains cholera germs because people who drink from it get cholera. At its most powerful a belief is a perception that forces us to look at the world in such a way that the perception is validated. If you believe someone to be nasty then your perception will select those aspects of behaviour which validate the belief. If you consider someone to be selfish then you will note those aspects of behaviour which convert your consideration into a belief. Plato's world view was itself a belief system. He believed that there were ultimate truths everywhere, just as there seemed to be in mathematics. If there was any difficulty in finding those truths then that was due to Socrates's proclaimed ignorance. This ignorance confirmed that the truths were there but could not be found.

Components always fit in around a belief system. A belief system is usually a good example of the self-organizing nature of information in the brain.

Belief systems are circular and therefore difficult to interrupt. They are not sustained by evidence in the outer world once they have been formed. Whatever the actual information in the outer world, perception will choose to structure it so as to support the belief.

The key operation in perception is 'flow'. This simply means that one event is succeeded by another. This aspect of flow is described in my book *Water Logic*. In that book I work with this concept of flow to produce 'flowscapes' which are an attempt to make visible to a person what might be going on in that person's perception. From the flowscape you can pick out what I call the 'collection points', the 'sensitive points' and the 'circular truths'.

All perceptual truth is probably 'circular'. In Figure 9 we can see how A leads to B which leads to C which leads to D which leads to E which leads to F which leads to D. The final circle is now established. It is difficult to see how perceptual truth could be anything other than circular. To explain a situation we go from situation to hypothesis and then run the hypothesis in our minds to find results which fit the existing situation. In science, proof is often no more than lack of imagination. If one explanation closes the circle we assume it must be the only one which could do that.

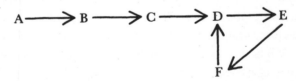

Figure 9

I have often complained that we need a simple, succinct word that would cover 'the way we look at the world at this moment'. That phrase is quite a mouthful. The word 'perception' is too broad, because it covers the whole process of looking at the world. The word 'perspective' indicates a position which might give rise to a particular point of view. The phrase 'logic bubble' comes close but relates more to the logical action that arises from the particular perception. By total chance a word suggested itself recently. In an article I had written there was a typing error which produced 'mypopic' instead of 'myopic'. This led to the possibility of using the word 'popic' to mean 'the way someone is looking at the situation at this moment'. The 'opic' part of the word is related to the Greek for eye. The 'p' or 'po' part can indicate 'possible' or 'potential'. The simplest way to remember the word would be as 'possible picture' of the world or 'popic'.

'Your popic sees unemployment as an inevitable factor in society.'

'My popic sees inadequate mechanisms for income transfer.'

'I believe his popic was that unemployment was a transitional state.'

'Your popic is very patchy and incomplete.'

'Lay out your popic alongside these others.'

At its most powerful a belief is a perception that forces us to look at the world in such a way that the perception is validated.

Why not just use the word 'view'? Because 'view' suggests an outcome opinion, whereas a popic is a sort of picture without an opinion attached. Will the word catch on? I doubt it.

What conclusions can we draw from this consideration of inner and outer worlds?

1. The inner world has been much neglected in favour of the 'objective' outer world.
2. The inner world has its own truth and its own logic which are different from those in the outer world.
3. The logic of the inner world tends to be 'water logic' rather than the 'rock logic' of the outer world.
4. The inner world contributes greatly to our thinking ability in terms of hypotheses, possibilities and concepts.

5. The beliefs of the inner world are not easily altered by reference to the outer world. There is a need to work in terms of inner-world logic.

6. The inner world is selective, subjective and fallible – but should not be neglected on that account.

7. Thought experiments are as valid as experiments in the outer world.

8. Traditional thinking is largely ineffective when dealing with inner-world behaviour. We need to develop more ways of dealing directly with perceptions.

9. Values, metaphors, models and objectives all exist in the inner world.

10. We may just need the new word 'popic' to describe 'a possible picture of the world around at this moment'.

27 ALTERNATIVES

Alternatives are, of course, a form of parallel thinking. The difference between alternatives and parallels is shown in Figure 10 overleaf. Alternatives are directed towards a single point. This may be the carrying out of a purpose: alternative material to make these cups from; alternative ways to reward successful salespeople; alternative ways to mark examination papers; alternative approaches to unemployment. There may also be a search for alternative ways of putting a particular concept into effect: alternative ways to discourage smoking; alternative ways to make people environmentally conscious; alternative ways to get participative democracy.

Parallels are simply items that are directed in the same general direction without the need to serve exactly the same purpose. They can include factors, ingredients, components, opinions, ideas, objections and requests all laid out alongside each other:

'Smokers could be given a discount if they attended a stop-smoking clinic.'

'Smokers contribute much to society through taxes and pension contributions that are not fully recovered.'

'A smoker's choice is no one else's business.'

'The need for the first puff is very important.'

'Some people do stop suddenly.'

'A sort of Smokers Anonymous on the lines of Alcoholics Anonymous might help.'

'A sense of achievement is important.'
'Badgering won't help.'
'It's your own business so long as others do not suffer.'
'It's important that youngsters are not pressured to start.'

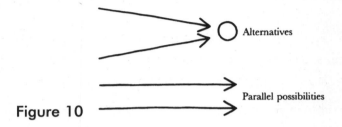

Figure 10

The above list is a very loose set of parallels on the general theme of 'discouraging smoking'. In practice this sort of discussion would be more productive with the use of a framework such as the Six Hats or the attention-directing tools of the CoRT programme. Otherwise there is the 'all-over-the-place' haphazardness that is typical of brainstorming. This means that there is insufficient attention to the various aspects. The real purpose of parallel thinking is to build up a full field of consideration, not to throw out ideas in a scattergun approach and hope that one works.

White hat (*information*)
What do we know about the age of starting smoking?
Do youngsters like the first cigarette?
Some people do stop suddenly.
How many smokers want to stop?

Green hat (*creative effort*)
Tobacco companies to run and profit from 'stop-smoking' clinics.
Very short cigarettes to counter first-puff craving.
'Show-off' badges for those who are stopping.
Cigarettes which do not upset your neighbours.

Yellow hat (*benefits*)
Tobacco companies would demonstrate 'free-choice' argument.
Each cigarette occasion would involve less smoking.
A sense of achievement is important.
Makes smoking your own business.

It is not surprising that in traditional thinking we are not at all keen to generate alternatives, because alternatives slow down the process of reaching the 'truth' or a certain conclusion.

Black hat (*caution*)
Shareholders would not like the idea.
You may end up smoking more cigarettes.
You would look 'smug'.
Technically probably not possible.

Red hat (*feelings*)
Too much pressure on smokers.
Need to make quitting easy.
Let smokers go their own way.
Youngsters should not start.

In this example the yellow and black hats were applied to the specific ideas generated under the green hat. The red hat applied to the whole theme.

Many books about problem-solving emphasize the importance of defining the problems in the 'right way'. This is somewhat dishonest, because the only time you can define the problem in the 'right way' is after you have solved the problem. Then you go back to say: 'If I had defined it this way, then the solution would have been easy.' This hindsight success is not of much practical value. Yet there is no doubt that some definitions of a problem are much more likely than others to lead to a solution.

The best we can do is to lay out parallel definitions of the problem and then to see the sort of thinking that follows from each definition.

Problem:
We do not have enough space in our car park.
Definitions of the problem:
There is not enough space for parking.
There is not enough space for those who want to park.
There are too many people who want to park in the car park.
There are too many people who feel they need to park in
   the car park.
There are too many people who have the use of the car park.
Cars are too large.
There is no further ground space to enlarge the car park.
We cannot provide more parking space.

From each definition may come ideas. For example, car parking might be restricted to the best performers in the previous week. Car pooling might be organized, or minibuses be provided. More space might be obtained by building layers upwards or below ground. Space might be obtained in someone else's car park. Parking might be restricted to small cars. Cars might be left in another car park and a shuttle service be operated. Car sharing might be enforced, with access to the car park only for those who got together.

**The real purpose of parallel thinking is to build up
a full field of consideration, not to throw out ideas in
a scattergun approach and hope that one works.**

How can you light a fire with something which must be cheap, does not carry any dangerous fuel, works fast and can also work at night? Such a tight definition virtually restricts the alternatives to a match. If the problem had been set more broadly then the replies might have included: lighter, match, solar reflector, rubbing two sticks together, etc. Is it better to have a tight definition to begin with or to have a broad definition and then to apply the constraints later to weed out those that do not apply? It is better to set the broad definition, for two reasons. The first reason is that often the boundaries can be challenged. The second reason is that it is better to generate many ideas and then to modify or exclude them than to have no ideas to work with.

It is apparent that there is a considerable overlap between 'alternatives' and 'parallels'. This is perfectly acceptable, because groupings in the parallel-thinking system are not hard-edged boxes with discrimination at the edges, but are more like flagpoles around which members of the 'class' cluster.

One of the main differences is that parallels are not seeking to arrive at a conclusion, whereas alternatives are always derived from some 'fixed point'. This fixed point may be a purpose: alternative ways of lighting a fire. It may be members of a class: alternative types of citrus fruit. It may be actualizations of a concept: alternative ways of carrying out the 'trading stamp' concept. Alternatives are like children of the same parents. You identify the parents and then you look for the siblings. What is the 'fixed point' here? How else can we reach that fixed point?

Strictly speaking an alternative means 'an other'. But if we proceed to find 'an other' for that other then alternatives can involve more than just two ways. In practice the number is unlimited. But the concept of 'an other' is important. Sometimes we reach the arrogance of certainty because we simply cannot imagine 'an other' possibility.

Some members of a group travelling together get a severe stomach upset.

'It must have been the meal we had last night. There is no other possibility. We use bottled water to clean our teeth and never drink tap water.' The certainty arises from an inability to see alternatives. As soon as an alternative is discovered then the certainty is reduced. That discovery will not come about through logic but through imagination. Of course, it will be logical in hindsight.

'What about the orange juices which some of us drank on the plane? Those could have been diluted with ordinary water. Or what about the ice some of us had in our whisky? How was that ice made?'

A clever and creative lawyer could probably put enough doubt into any jury's mind to make it difficult to convict 'beyond reasonable doubt'.

It is not surprising that in traditional thinking we are not at all keen to generate alternatives, because alternatives slow down the process of reaching the 'truth' or a certain conclusion. The more alternatives, the slower the process. The more alternatives, the less certainty about the conclusion.

28 PARALLELS

It is interesting to note that Aristotle remarked that Socrates used 'parallels' in bringing forth examples of 'justice' or whatever else he wanted to define, in order to try to extract the true definition from considerations of these examples. This is the classic operation of induction. 'How can we find the hidden truth?'

The main characteristic of parallel thinking is that when we generate parallels and lay them alongside each other we are not, at that point, trying to come to any conclusion. We are just looking in a defined direction. There is no question of true/false. There is no question of refutation. There is no selection of 'good examples'. There is no question of statements being contradictory. With induction there has to be a careful 'choice' of examples, otherwise the process cannot work. If you want to define the 'essence' of a hound then your collection of dogs must only include 'hounds'. If you allow in terriers and toy poodles then you are never going to be able to use induction to arrive at a conclusion. Paradoxically, induction presupposes some prior definition which selects the examples permitted into the ring for evaluation.

If you allowed only white swans into your examples of 'swan' then you would conclude that swans were always white. If you used other characteristics as a basis for allowing in examples then you might conclude that swans could be black or white.

There is an interesting circularity in the whole process of induction. The important point, however, is that there is selection of examples. In parallel thinking there is no selection at all.

In Figure 11 we see an overhead view of some people looking at a building. They are all looking at the same side. They are looking in the same direction. They are looking in parallel. They report, in parallel, on what they see.

In Figure 12 each of the people is looking at a different side of the building. They report in parallel, and each report is laid alongside the other reports.

In Figure 13 each person is now looking at a different building in the same village. Once again they report in parallel.

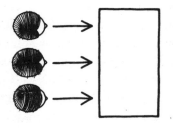

Figure 11

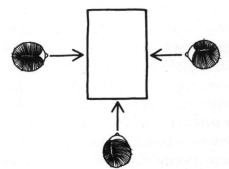

Figure 12

Figure 13

In each of the three instances 'parallel' thinking (or seeing) is taking place. The difference is in the 'theme' or 'direction'.

In one case there are parallel views of one side of the building.

In another case there are parallel views of the whole building.

In another case there are parallel views of the village.

The subject under discussion or under thought determines the theme or direction. This need not be defined very tightly. Nevertheless there are grades of relevance. If irrigation is being discussed then the charms of a particular pop singer may not be relevant – unless brought in specifically as a 'provocation'. At what point does something cross over from being relevant to being irrelevant? There is no sharp line and no discriminating judgement to be made. If you ask a group of people to look north, some of them will be very accurate and others so inaccurate as to be looking almost west. Where is the discriminating line? Is it between north-east and north-west?

While it is important to guide and comment on relevance, there is no need to use harsh rejection. Those parallels which are less relevant will be less useful and less used when it comes to designing the way forward from the parallels. As I indicated in a previous section, there is not the judge/gatekeeper that is so strong a part of traditional thinking.

It might also be said that, as with induction, if we prejudge relevance too sharply we shall be predetermining what we then 'find'. If I permit only 'orange-coloured' fruits into my discussion on citrus fruits then I may come to conclusions that apply only to orange-coloured citrus fruits. It is better to be broad first and narrow later. This is no problem at all with parallel thinking, which is not based on initial judgements. With traditional thinking, however, it is a huge problem, because there has to be an initial judgement most of the time.

Someone once remarked that prospective homebuyers should always view houses in winter. In summer the leaves on a tree might obscure the view of the gasworks. Should the parallel views of the building all be obtained on the same day and under the same conditions? They need not be so uniform unless a certain context is actually specified in the subject direction. As with alternatives, it is sometimes best to have a broad direction first and then later to narrow it down or even divide it into subdirections.

For those brought up in traditional thinking methods, this lack of entry-point judgement is disconcerting, because they feel that lack of judgement must mean irrelevance. That is because of the relevant/irrelevant dichotomy they hold in their heads. The spectrum from highly relevant to irrelevant is obviously a smooth one – as suggested earlier.

In the section on alternatives, I commented upon the difference between structured and unstructured parallel thinking. In unstructured parallel thinking there is just the description of the subject theme or direction. All comments aimed in that broad direction are accepted and are laid down alongside each other. With structured parallel thinking, however, there is a defined 'subframe' which also sets a direction. For example, if the general subject is 'agricultural subsidies' and the subframe is 'yellow hat' then, for the moment, the thinkers 'direct their attention' to the perceived possible benefits and values in agricultural subsidies – such as preserving a rural way of life with small farmers.

**In traditional adversarial thinking the justification
for each statement is sought when that statement is
made. In parallel thinking, any 'possibility' is accepted
as such.**

On a minor point, it may be argued that in real life you cannot
look in two directions at the same time. But, in a way, you
can. Imagine you are looking at a building. Without shifting
your gaze you now put on some rose-tinted spectacles and
note what you see. Then you put on some yellow spectacles
and note what you see. If the building is multicoloured your
different 'views' will be different. It is in this sense that the
subframes of structured parallel thinking work. In practice
they work very easily and very well. They remove confusion
and make parallel exploration much more powerful than in
the unstructured approach to parallel thinking.

I want to repeat a point I made in an earlier section, because
it is such an important point. With parallel thinking we set out to
look in a defined direction. It is this sense of directing attention
and seeking to look in that direction which is so important. It
is not a matter of 'classifying' observations after they have been
made. It is not a matter of making sundry remarks and then classifying them as 'problems', 'benefits', etc. In practice, and in the
way the brain works, the difference between the two is huge. One
process is a directing of attention; the other process is a judgement
classification of results. Those accustomed to traditional thinking
will often confuse the two.

The whole point about 'directing attention' is that you may
not 'see' something unless you have directed your attention
that way. Merely classifying what you have found has no effect
whatsoever on helping you to 'see' better.

Once again we can underline the difference between the
Socratic method and parallel thinking. In the Socratic method

and traditional thinking we assume that, somehow, the ideas, statements, observations and perceptions 'are there'. Somehow they arrive. Somehow they come into being. All that we have to do is to judge them and to classify them. That is the essence of critical thinking. But where do these perceptions, observations, statements and ideas come from? How are they generated? It is easy enough, in school, to present them in textbooks. It is easy enough in a Socratic dialogue to have the other party suggest something. But in real life the deficiency is as much on the generative side as on the judgement side. That is why the directing of attention in parallel thinking is so important. Socratic questioning is a much weaker system and is only really applicable to the 'meaning' of words and terms.

The first part of parallel thinking is therefore generative in nature.

One of the most striking differences between the Socratic method and parallel thinking is the treatment of contradictions. As I have already discussed, it is a fundamental of Western logic that something cannot 'be' and 'not be' at the same time. In a sense the whole of Aristotelian logic pivots on this point. This rejection of contradiction means that we can accept the box system of 'categories'. Something belongs in a category or it does not belong. It could not both belong and not belong. This applies to classes, groups, sets, etc. In the Socratic dialogues, Socrates uses contradiction as an argument device. 'If we accept this and this then we come to this contradiction – so it could not be so.'

In the *Phaedo,* Socrates says: 'There is no compatibility in the two propositions that the soul is simply the harmony of the body as a tune is the harmony of a lyre and the proposition that knowledge is recollection of something that is already there.' In one case the knowledge is already there but in the other case it comes only after the body has come into existence. The two propositions are incompatible or mutually exclusive. This means that the harmony idea has to be rejected, because the 'knowledge is recollection' idea can be 'proved'.

In many arguments in politics and in law, one party seeks to bring the other to the point where a contradiction is being offered or asserted. At that point the other side has obviously failed and is 'wrong'. The non-acceptance of contradictions is a sort of 'game truth' based on language. If we define a table as 'having four legs' then we simply cannot accept a table with three legs. If the object does not have four legs we cannot 'call it' a table. For the sake of communication clarity in sequential languages (as distinct from overlapping languages) this habit is necessary.

In parallel thinking, contradictions are fully accepted. This is because the emphasis is not on 'what is' but on 'what happens next' and 'what does this lead to' ('water logic' rather than 'rock logic').

'The plane to Paris leaves at 16.00.'

'The plane to Paris leaves at 17.00.'

These seem to be mutually exclusive. They are contradictory if we convert them into the form:

'The plane to Paris is scheduled to leave at 16.00.'

'The plane to Paris is not scheduled to leave at 16.00.'

This is because a contradiction is limited to 'is' and 'is not'.

We accept both statements in parallel. Then when it comes to 'designing the way forward' we can check them out by telephoning or looking up the timetable. It may be that the two statements are not even contradictory, because planes go at both times or because both times are right on different days. If we cannot check the time then we design an action that encompasses both. We get to the airport in time for the 16.00 flight and, if that is incorrect, we sit and read a de Bono book until the 17.00 flight.

In this simple example we see first of all that what seems to be a contradiction may actually turn out not to be a contradiction at all. There is therefore the danger of instantly rejecting what appear to be contradictions on present evidence but which turn out not to be contradictions at all. Then there is the matter of checking statements at the time they need to be checked – not at the time of entry into the system. Finally, we can design an action that encompasses both possibilities. This is similar to the well-known process of 'scenario building' as a way of looking into the future. We imagine the best case and the worst case and then we design a course of action that would be suitable at both extremes and also in between.

In parallel thinking, contradictions are fully accepted.

There is an important further point that needs to be added. The contradictory opinions about the time of the plane might have led to a lot of irrelevant argument at that point. The contradiction might have been an excuse for power politics in which one person sought to prove another person inaccurate. None of that is possible with parallel thinking.

If parallel thinking is not particular about who is allowed into the 'party', then where does 'truth' come in? The answer is that truth comes in when we need it. Truth comes in when we need to design or check out a proposed action. Truth comes in when we have the whole picture.

'Salt is good on food.'

'Salt is not good on food.'

These two statements are contradictory. Which one should we let into the 'party'? If you had to make that 'gatekeeper' judgement you would be wrong whichever way you judged. If both statements are let into the party then, later, we can try to reconcile them. We might come to the conclusion that some salt is good but too much salt is bad. We might come to the conclusion that some people believe that salt is bad for you if you have high blood pressure. On the other hand, if you are in a hot climate then salt is good because you lose so much in sweat. It is only when you have the whole picture that judgement can be offered. Piecemeal, gateway judgement is bound to be inadequate in some cases.

In the first stage, parallel thinking is not seeking uniformity, agreement or conclusions. Nor is there a search for objective truth. The emphasis is on possibilities and popics (possible pictures).

The key phrase in parallel thinking is 'laying down alongside'. Each contribution is carefully laid down alongside the others. There is no interaction between the contributions. This is totally contrary to traditional adversarial thinking, in which every statement is an occasion for judgement and attack. At first, those trained in traditional adversarial thinking find it very hard to restrain themselves when someone else in a group puts forward a statement with which they do not agree or which seems to be 'wrong'. There is a strong tendency to pounce on that statement, to show that it is wrong and to indicate that the person putting it forward is 'foolish'.

It is to restrain this tendency that the Six Hats parallel-thinking framework was designed. The 'rules' of the game of the hats serve to prevent this instant attack and instant judgement.

In the laying down of parallels, agreement is not required. It is enough that each statement or contribution falls within the general subject area (and the subframe, where this is in use). Parallels offered on the causes of ethnic conflict might include:

'Deep-seated and historical hatreds which have been suppressed in the past can now come to the surface (as in the former Yugoslavia).'

'In times of chaos, confusion and uncertainty, tribal groups intensify their identity because it provides a sense of order and also indicates the enemies.'

'It is a matter of moment-to-moment continuity. There are rumours of attack or atrocity. The need to defend your group. The empowerment of your defenders. The danger of being regarded as a traitor.'

'There is banditry and criminality, and the ethnic divisions are just a way of legitimizing this.'

'A lack of hope, purpose or possibility of achievement leads to conflict being the only sort of motivating activity, leading to warlords and local fighting. This is the new area of entrepreneurship.'

'Confusion leads to a necessity for a sense of belonging. It is also necessary to have some clan to look after your interests. So group identity gets stronger and stronger. This is helped by the need to identify and hate other groups.'

'All the positive-feedback loops are towards escalation and continuity of the conflict. In this situation the slightest thing can trigger a major conflict.'

'It is simply extremely difficult to stop, because the peer group puts pressure on anyone who wants to stop – and there is uncertainty about whether the "other side" will also stop.'

'Each side comes to see the conflict as "self-defence" against real or imagined aggression by the other side.'

'There is an impossibility of a middle ground. Each person is forced into the sharp dichotomy of "with us" or "against us". Perceptually, no middle ground can exist.'

'Tit-for-tat revenge and reaction create each incident, and the chain of incidents becomes the conflict. There is no overall plan or strategy.'

'Individual warlords enjoy the power, position, importance and camaraderie that arise from the conflict and so wish to continue the conditions which give rise to these benefits.'

Which of these possibilities is true? All of them, none of them, some of them, or parts of each?

Parallel thinking allows all of them to be put down in parallel. There is no need to discuss and argue about each one as it is suggested. In traditional adversarial thinking the justification for each statement is sought when that statement is made. In the 'possibility' atmosphere of parallel thinking, any 'possibility' is accepted as such. Because there is no claim for 'truth', there is no need to resist or seek to refute a suggestion. The suggestion comes to exist as a 'possibility' among other possibilities.

There is often an unstated fear that if remote possibilities are allowed in alongside very likely possibilities then the remote ones will be elevated to a status they do not deserve. The feeling is that all possibilities are not equal and therefore should not be treated as equal. In a horse race it is theoretically possible for any one of the entrants to win, but any punter knows that some horses are much more likely to win than others. So why treat them as equal possibilities? Why not put some sort of odds against each possibility? The answer is that it is not a horse race and the analogy is inappropriate. If you walk around a building there are different perspectives. It is true that the facade is the one most likely to get noticed, but all the perspectives come together to give a total view. So it is never a matter of 'choosing' which of the parallels is the most likely to be 'true' as in choosing the horse most likely to win. All the parallels contribute to the overall picture. It is from all the parallels that the outcome will be designed. So the analogy of the horse race is inappropriate.

A piece of woven cloth may contain parallel fibres which are all of the same colour. Or some of the fibres may be of a different colour. Some of these colours will contribute much more strongly to the overall pattern or attractiveness of the cloth. Yet each fibre contributes equally to the cloth as such. It is very similar with parallels. Each contributes to the overall picture or 'field'. Yet some of the contributions are more likely or more powerful than others. In a picture, the background has as much a role to play as the foreground. In a scene, the shadows give form to the objects.

The most important point in parallel thinking is to realize that you are not proceeding sequentially from one 'true' statement to the next until a conclusion is reached. Instead, the possibilities are laid out in parallel and then the outcome is 'designed' – as we shall see in a later section.

29 POSSIBILITIES

Traditional Western thinking – the Socratic method, the Gang of Three – operates with 'truth'. This implies certainty and absolutes. It was Plato's fascist contribution to insist on there being these absolutes which Socrates was then asked to find – in Plato's dialogues. As I indicated in a previous section, we are not sure whether Plato's ideas were influenced by Socrates or whether Socrates's behaviour made him into a convenient mouthpiece for Plato. It does not much matter. The end result, which was polished up by Aristotle, was the judgement/box system. Something is 'in' a particular box or it is 'out'.

All this leads to our usual logic, which has to work with 'all', 'none', 'always' and 'never'.

'All snails have shells.'

'This snail-like creature does not have a shell.'

'So this is not a snail.'

If we get away from the hard absolutes, the system loses its force:

'Snails very often have shells.'

'This snail-like creature does not have a shell.'

'So this is probably not a snail.'

But it 'could be' – that is not excluded. Both science and day-to-day logic are much more comfortable with certainty. If this is the certainty of 'game truth', where we decide what we call things ('I shall only call snails those snail-like creatures with shells'), there is no problem. The problem arises when we seek to apply this to 'experience truth' and the world around.

As soon as we step away from 'all', 'always', 'none' and 'never' to 'usually', 'sometimes', 'by and large' and 'some' then we are in the world of 'possibility'.

Possibility is at the heart of parallel thinking. Since there is to be no gatekeeper judgement as to 'truth', matters can never rise above being 'possibilities'. No truth test has been applied; no truth claim can therefore be made. The intention is that from the 'field' enriched with parallel possibilities an outcome will 'organize itself' or be consciously 'designed'.

Figure 14 shows what a child might do with some solid wooden cubes. Each cube might be placed squarely on top of the cube below and a stable tower would be built. This is similar to traditional thinking. Because 'truth' is claimed for each step, step by step the structure will be built and it will be stable.

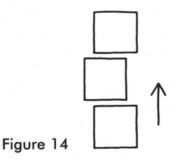

Figure 14

If we replace truth with 'possibility' as suggested in Figure 15 then we cannot proceed in this way. The pieces are not stable. We need only one piece to be unstable for the whole structure to collapse. Without absolutes at each point in a logical argument there is no confidence in the conclusion.

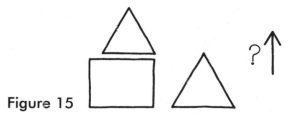

Figure 15

But we can lay even spherical pieces out on the ground and design an outcome from them, as suggested in Figure 16. This is what parallel thinking is about.

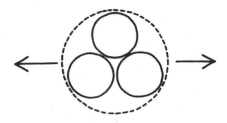

Figure 16

In our minds, 'possibility' always has a strong relationship with 'probability'. 'Yes, this is indeed possible – but is it likely?'

With parallel thinking it is best to stay away from fine-tuning of probability. This is because as soon as we give a probability grading then we are edging back to a weaker form of truth. We are edging back to saying: 'This is not absolutely true but it is likely' or 'This is not absolutely false but it is likely.' As a result, the thinking operation ends up being a probability assessment operation rather than a 'design' operation.

Instead of seeking to set probabilities for each possibility, it is enough to operate within a broad spectrum of possibilities:

Realistic possibilities (reasonably probable).

Remote possibilities (just possible).

Fantasy possibilities (the mind can conceive of them, that is all).

Provocation (not possible at all but used to provoke ideas).

There is no need actively to use this gradation: the possibilities will define themselves. Because we are not dealing with the truth system, at this stage the actual contribution that a 'possible parallel' makes to the final outcome will eventually depend on its likelihood value. This does not have to be assessed upfront. At the same time it is useful if the thinkers do not spend all their time contributing fantasy-type possibilities. That may have a value in a traditional brainstorming session but not in parallel thinking. In practice people quickly get to understand the idiom of parallel thinking, the rules of the game. The greatest difficulty is with those who are used to brainstorming and fail to see that parallel thinking is not brainstorming just because there is no immediate judgement. It is difficult to do productive parallel thinking with such people.

The intention is that from the 'field' enriched with parallel possibilities an outcome will 'organize itself' or be consciously 'designed'.

What sort of things does 'possibility' cover? There is a whole range of matters. The list given below is not comprehensive. Also the items on the list overlap – which is, of course, permitted in parallel thinking.

1. Things we believe to be true but cannot be sure. 'Swans are usually white.' 'I believe there are no death duties in Queensland.'
2. A defined matter of chance. 'If I throw these dice the numbers may add up to 11.' 'If I pull the trigger of this revolver there is a one in six chance I might shoot myself.'
3. Possible connections. 'Your tummy upset might be due to the curry you had for lunch.' 'There is a possibility the luggage-handlers opened your case and stole the camera.'

4. Future prediction. 'The economy might recover next year.' 'There might be a better grape harvest next year.'
5. True for some. 'Some schizophrenics can become violent.' 'Some taxi drivers are brilliant conversationalists.'
6. Under certain circumstances. 'There can be accidents at this point if the road is wet.' 'If you eat too much sugar you could get reactive hypoglycaemia.'
7. Alternative explanations. 'The missing wallet could have been stolen, but it might have been lost or simply mislaid.' 'She has either forgotten the appointment, lost her way or got caught up in traffic.'
8. Scientific hypotheses. 'A possible explanation for the spider's ability to jump is a high-pressure hydraulic system.' 'The high incidence of Aids may be due to a more contagious form of the virus.'
9. Possible recognition. 'This painting could possibly be by Corot.' 'I think your son may have measles.'
10. Possible courses of action (or decision). 'We could do nothing, or we could cease operations, or we could move abroad.' 'You could forget it, take him to court or go punch him on the nose.'
11. Possible changes. 'It is possible that people's taste is changing.' 'It is possible that people are less interested in sport today.'
12. Possible outcomes. 'If we lower prices we might get a higher hotel occupancy rate.' 'If you use distilled water your plants might grow better.'

The situations on the above list overlap a great deal. It would have been possible to categorize 'possibilities' more succinctly under such headings as: 'incomplete information', 'speculation', 'unconfirmed application', 'defined chances', etc. This might have been neater but less practical in value.

In a previous section I suggested a simple definition of truth as the opposite of any situation in which you might say 'not so'. We can define possibility as any situation in which you could say 'maybe so'.

It should be obvious that parallel thinking does not exclude truth. If you read the correct timetable and declare that the train for London leaves from the station at 15.00, you are not prevented from contributing that as a parallel. Many contributions will be ones which the thinker knows or believes to be true. Parallel thinking is not restricted to 'possibilities'. So should you indicate that your contribution is 'true' in order to give it more value and in order to distinguish it from the other mere possibilities? The temptation to do so is great. Yet the claim to 'truth' could lead to that claim being disputed there and then. So it is better to make a simple statement.

'My timetable, which I have in front of me, says that the train leaves at 15.00.'

'I often catch this train and it leaves at 15.00.'

'My secretary checked the train times earlier this morning and the London train leaves at 15.00.'

From such simple statements the 'truth' value can be inferred without having to be claimed directly. The listeners can then decide how to treat the contribution.

You are driving along and you come to a fork in the road. The road sign has been defaced. There are two possibilities: you could drive right or you could drive left. There are two possible choices: you could decide to drive right or you could decide to drive left. This seems very obvious. But it is not true. In fact you have several more possibilities.

You could drive right.

You could drive left.

You could stop to think further.

You could consult your map.

You could wait for someone to come and then ask.

You could decide to take a risk.

You could go back to the previous junction and try another route.

There probably are further possibilities that might be added to this list. That is perfectly 'possible'.

We can define possibility as any situation in which you could say 'maybe so'.

With our usual habit of dichotomy thinking we love to close the door on possibilities in order to give us the needed certainty for getting on with things. We feel that there is a real danger of being paralysed by possibilities – and there is such a danger. But there is no need to be paralysed by possibilities if we have a clear sense of priorities and practicalities. We simply look at the possibilities and 'design' the way forward. It would be difficult to obtain the full set of possibilities in every situation, but we should be able to do better than a simple either/or.

You might be inclined to throw up your hands and say that everything is 'possible'. The mugger who attacks you in the street 'might' die of a heart attack there and then. The big man walking on the opposite side of the street 'might' come to your rescue. A police car 'might' be passing at the moment. The mugger 'might' like your friendly face and go mug elsewhere. All these are 'possibilities', but they would not help you very much. But if you considered that you might get mugged in a certain part of the city, or that the mugger might get violent, or that the mugger might be on drugs, then such possibilities could have a practical effect.

It is simply a matter of looking forward with the flow of water logic. One set of possibilities does nothing except say: 'Hope for the best.' The other set of possibilities suggests practical guidelines for action.

Very often it is our habitual concern for 'what is' which makes us want to 'judge' possibilities. As soon as we switch to 'what can be' then this difficulty disappears. The difficulty arises from being half in the traditional thinking system and half in the parallel-thinking system. That means that we accept possibilities (new system) but then want to 'judge' them (old system).

It must be obvious by now that the 'possibility' stage of parallel thinking is the productive stage. This is the generative stage. This is the creative stage.

I have sought to emphasize at various points in this book that the traditional thinking system is extremely weak on the generative side. In traditional thinking the emphasis has been on criticism, judgement, analysis and the search for the truth. Very little of this is generative. It is assumed that ideas will somehow emerge. It is assumed that the 'truth' is there to be discovered.

The generative or productive side of thinking demands 'possibilities'. There have to be possibilities before they can be assessed. Parallel thinking deliberately encourages such possibility thinking.

Under parallel thinking comes the whole area of creative thinking. I have not mentioned this until this point because I did not want to give the impression that parallel thinking is just to do with creative and lateral thinking. That is certainly not the case. None of the parallels needs to be creative. They can all be sound suggestions, hypotheses and pieces of information.

At the same time, new possibilities, new ideas, new hypotheses and new solutions can be generated either by the simple intention to be creative or through the formal creative methods of lateral thinking. Any new idea is a 'possibility'. Such an idea may be developed further. Eventually the idea will take part in the design of the outcome. Sometimes the idea itself is impractical but from it may be extracted a valuable concept which can indeed be used.

In structured parallel thinking the new idea possibilities would be put forward under the green hat. Where the thinking is unstructured they may emerge at any time.

'Why not create a joint force crossing the ethnic divide?'

'Could we break the continuity?'

'Could we buy-off the warlords and make it to their advantage to desist?'

'How could we set up a middle position to break the sharp dichotomy?'

Questions are ways of focusing creative effort. 'How could we break the continuity?' means 'Let us focus creative effort on ways of breaking the continuity.' Among the parallels there may be suggestions for further focusing of the thinking.

So, when we have all the parallel possibilities, what do we do next? What happens next? To many traditionalists this phase of laying out possibilities will seem self-indulgent and impractical. The purpose of thinking is enjoyment, understanding, control or prediction. How can a mass of unjudged possibilities help? With traditional thinking we would by now have been moving steadily along towards an outcome through a series of carefully judged 'truth steps'. Instead we have a soup of possibilities. Now what?

30 DESIGNING A WAY FORWARD

If thinking is going to serve its various purposes then we need to move forward from the field of 'parallel possibilities' to the desired outcome. This is where 'design' comes in.

In a previous section I contrasted design with analysis. I indicated that analysis is concerned with 'what is', whereas design is concerned with 'what can be'. I indicated that the traditional search for the 'truth' is like prospecting for gold. Worthy as this may sometimes be, it is not the same as designing and constructing a house. You are not going to 'discover' a house – you have to make it happen.

In general, use of the term 'design' is sometimes restricted to graphic design, theatre design, dress design, industrial design, etc. Very often these aspects of design deal with the visual aspect, though the functional aspect is also important. Design is often seen to be a cousin of 'art'. In this book I am using the word 'design' in the broad and strong sense in which I believe it should be used. For me, design is 'bringing something into being to serve a purpose'. While design may be creative, it does not have to be. The emphasis is on making something happen. It is not enough just to judge, criticize, refute and search. You actually have to *do* something.

I have sought to show in this book that our traditional thinking system in its obsession with the 'search for the truth' has paid insufficient attention to developing the thinking skills needed for design. Society cannot thrive on judgement alone. In times of rapid change like the present, the need for design is more important than ever. Judgement may just be enough to resist change but not enough to benefit from change.

In this section I shall be dealing with design in a narrower sense: how we design an outcome from the field of parallel possibilities.

Traditional Western thinking, in its pure form, does not have or need a design stage. Each step follows the last step with a judgement as to whether the step is true/false, right/wrong. It is like a mason making sure that each stone is squarely and truly based on the preceding stone: 'If this is so then this is so.' In practice, of course, the purity of the traditional thinking method is contaminated by various attempts to generate alternatives, etc. This is regarded as 'somehow happening', often aided by a simplistic analysis which assumes that you can either do something or not do it.

Society cannot thrive on judgement alone. Judgement may just be enough to resist change but not enough to benefit from change.

With parallel thinking the design stage is very important, because without it the parallel-possibility stage has only a small value.

Several things may happen in the design stage of parallel thinking:

1. The outcome becomes obvious.
2. The outcome organizes itself.
3. The outcome needs to be designed deliberately.

If you go to a store to buy some clothes you may look through a variety of styles and try on different sizes. If you have to make a decision you will need to consider price, utility, colour, style, practicality, size, etc. This is the hard way of making a choice. Occasionally, however, you find exactly what you want: right style, right colour, right size and right price. The same often applies to buying a house. Usually you have to try to convince yourself to buy the most practical choice. Once again you consider all the factors. Occasionally you fall in love with a house at first sight. There are those who claim that marriage can also happen in either of those two ways: careful assessment or instant love.

The same thing can happen with the parallel possibilities. The desired outcome can spring directly, and without further consideration, from the field of parallel possibilities. It may depend on one of the possibilities or on a simple combination of possibilities.

Your travel agent tells you of the different ways you could get from Malta to Mexico City. One of them stands out as being obviously the best.

A good map of a holiday country helped by advice from the locals will lay out the 'landscape' of the tour you want to make. Designing the best route may be easy. Thinking is not always difficult. Thinking does not have to be difficult.

Traditional thinking often makes things much more difficult than they need to be, because traditional thinking is so poor at generating options and possibilities. It is far easier to select from a wide range of possibilities than to reason your way to a good choice.

In practice, it is surprising how often the structured parallel thinking of the Six Hats method leads directly to a decision or outcome without any conscious design effort. The outcome seems obvious when the possibilities have been laid out.

The second way in which the field of parallel possibilities can proceed to a useful outcome is through the process of 'self-organizing'. This is an unusual concept for those who believe that nothing happens unless at every moment we are making it happen. The more we know about the brain, the more we come to realize that in at least some of its behaviour it is a self-organizing information system. That means that information organizes itself into patterns, flows and outcomes. Those interested in these particular aspects could read about them in my other books.*

Rain falling on to a virgin landscape eventually organizes itself into streams, tributaries and a river. The river gets to the sea. In exactly the same way, input laid out as parallel possibilities can sometimes organize itself into an outcome. Sometimes two 'rivers' form and there is a double outcome. We then have to choose between the two.

In life, designers and artists sometimes work this way. They saturate their minds with the different ingredients, needs and possibilities and then wait for everything to organize itself into an outcome.

To help this process, we just read through the field of parallel possibilities over and over again and wait for some outcome to start forming. The process is not as rapid or as complete as with the instant outcome mentioned previously.

There may be a stage in which a general concept forms and this gradually refines down into a practical outcome.

In the future we shall certainly have computer software which will allow a field of parallel possibilities to organize itself into a useful outcome. Along with others, I am working on just such software. In a sense, today's neural-network computers do that by allowing experience over time to organize itself as a way of processing information.

There are some simple and easy-to-use techniques which we can apply in order to help possibilities to organize themselves.

* *The Mechanism of Mind* (London: Vermilion, 2015) and *I am Right, You are Wrong*.

One such technique is the 'flowscape' technique.* This is directly based on 'water logic' and how one perception flows to another.

A simple flowscape can be constructed around some of the notions put forward in this book.

A Judgement is not enough. *B*
B There has to be something to be judged. *C*
C The generation of ideas is important. *I*
D We are complacent about our judgement system. *E*
E The system is good at defending itself within its own rules. *D*
F Generation of ideas involves possibility. *G*
G Possibilities need to interact. *H*
H Design can only be judged as a whole. *B*
I Both idea-generation and design are needed. *A*
J 'What is' does not ensure 'what can be'. *E*

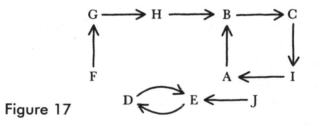

Figure 17

Each possibility is simply connected to one other possibility. The resulting flowscape is shown in Figure 17. At once it becomes obvious that, in the thinking of the person constructing the flowscape, the judgement system is content to defend itself and disregards the need for ideas. We can also see that what is to be judged depends on both idea-generation and the design process. The flowscape makes visible a structure in the thinking. Sometimes this is obvious; often it produces a new

---

* See my book *Water Logic*.

insight. Is this flowscape 'true'? It may give a reasonable picture of the thinking of the person making the flowscape, but even that is not certain.

But the important question to ask is not 'Is it true?' but 'What happens next?' The answer to this question may be highly useful and practical. There is no point in trying to attack a system that is valid and content within its own framework. The best approach is to show how the system is excellent but inadequate on the generative and constructive side of thinking.

One of the functions of the flowscape is to suggest the key points and the sensitive points. These are the points that contribute most. We can then focus attention on these points. For example, we would need to check out these points. Are they valid? This is much simpler than checking out all points when some of them contribute very little.

Design is concerned with the following types of consideration:

'What does this contribute?'

'Can these be "combined"?'

'What are the values and concepts?'

'Is this valid?'

'What does the outcome lead to?'

Design may have more than one stage. In one-stage design we go straight from the field of parallel possibilities to an outcome. In two-stage design we may go from the field of parallel possibilities to some alternatives and then proceed to choose from the alternatives. In three-stage design we may first establish some concepts, then form some alternatives and finally make a choice between the alternatives. There is no need at all to categorize these different sequences: it is enough to realize that sometimes you cannot go straight to the outcome.

The first step in design is usually one of comparison. We look across the parallel possibilities to see how they compare one with the other.

We look for similarities. Some of the possibilities may be saying the same thing in a different way. Some are complementary or supplementary to each other. Some may focus on a broad concept, and others on a particular example of the same concept. This consideration of similarities may lead to the emergence of a more general concept which covers many of the possibilities. There is no pressure to achieve this – the exercise is not one of 'grouping' possibilities – but such a concept may emerge naturally and can then take its place in the field as a possibility.

In contrast to the great readiness of traditional thinking to throw out one side of the contradiction, in the design process we seek to extract maximum value from both sides of any contradiction.

After considering similarities we can focus on differences. These may vary from a difference of emphasis to possibilities that are contradictory, mutually exclusive and totally incompatible. We explore the basis for the difference. Perhaps it is looking at a different part of the same picture. Perhaps the circumstances or context might be different.

'He is a smoker.'

'He is not a smoker.'

It turns out that he smokes at home but never in the office. The two mutually exclusive statements turn out to be perfectly compatible.

After examining and seeking to understand the differences, there is an attempt to see if they can coexist. It is not a matter of choosing between them or establishing which one is true and which one is false. The key question is: 'What do they contribute to the possible outcome?'

An attempt is made to reconcile out-and-out contradictions. Are both positions valid but at different times, under different circumstances or for different people? Can both be used? Is it not possible to use both a carrot and a stick?

In contrast to the great readiness of traditional thinking to throw out one side of the contradiction, in the design process we seek to extract maximum value from both sides of any contradiction.

Sometimes we may need to create a third or further concept to embrace both the contradictory concepts. For example, to embrace both 'carrot' and 'stick' we might have the concept 'inducements to change present behaviour'. Carrot and stick now become alternative ways of carrying through that concept. A worker may leave a company and not leave a company. The worker can retire but immediately come back as a consultant.

The creation of new concepts is very much part of the design process. Sometimes the new concept can be expressed neatly. At other times it may be expressed as a phrase, such as 'some way of separating the strongly motivated from those who just go along'. We then seek ways of bringing it about.

We can express a need as 'something' or 'some way'.

'We need some way of giving benefit to those who park outside the city centre.'

'We need something to prevent cars heating up in the sun.'

'We need some way of communicating with the local leaders.'

If we cannot reconcile contradictions and cannot show one side to be invalid, then we proceed to design an outcome which covers both possibilities.

'We cannot decide whether he is competent for this job or not. We can give him a trial period, we can monitor his progress closely, we can give him a competent assistant, etc.'

In practice, once you reject the either/or choices of traditional thinking, contradictions are not as great a difficulty as they may seem.

After comparison, we may proceed to extract values and concepts. Sometimes we may want to do this before the comparison stage. Sometimes we may have the comparison stage, then extract concepts and values and then compare again.

Some possibilities may already have been expressed in concept form. From almost anything that has been offered as a parallel it is possible to extract one or more concepts. You can even go from a concept to a broader concept. From the concept of 'road metering', in which an electronic device records how much road a car has used during a given period, we can go to the broader concept of charging cars by their use.

In the design process, concepts are much easier to deal with than detail. You cannot change detail but you can change concepts. You can make a concept broader, you can modify a concept, you can combine concepts. For example, there is no need to list every single flight from London to Paris. It is enough to talk of 'a regular and convenient air service between London and Paris'.

Skill in working with concepts is essential for the design process. Concepts are groupings and organizations of experience which allow us to see things in a certain way and to seek for certain types of action. If you are looking for 'food', you are more likely to find something to eat than if you are looking only for 'a bar of chocolate'. And if you are looking only for 'a bar of Cadbury's milk chocolate' your chances will be even less.

Creativity can come in at any point in the design process. There can also be defined creative needs: 'We need a new idea to limit the mobility of teenagers in order to reduce crime.' The creative need can be pinpointed and then the techniques of lateral thinking[*] can be used in a formal and deliberate way to generate new concepts and new ideas. During the design process it is worth pinpointing areas of creative need: 'We need some way of reducing street begging.' That becomes a creative

---

[*] See my book *Serious Creativity*.

focus. The outcome of the creative effort is added into the design process.

To be useful, a designed outcome must have a 'value'. From where does this value come? It comes from the values involved in the situation – and these include the different values of the different parties involved – and from the values of the group or person doing the thinking. In the case of an agreed problem then the value of the solution rests on its ability to solve the problem. Has the problem been removed?

This sense of 'value' is constantly present during the design process, but it is not used as an accept/reject criterion for every suggestion. It is part of the design process.

A fundamental aspect of the design process is to extract the values of the parties involved. In the case of a conflict, there are the values of those involved directly, the values of those caught up in the conflict, the values of third parties, etc. In negotiation, the values of those involved are central to the whole process. The different parties have different values. Successful negotiation means designing an outcome which satisfies the different values. Occasionally it may be useful to design and insert a 'new value'. Values such as 'gain', 'security', 'flexibility', 'status', 'recognition', 'dignity' are all important. How do these contribute to the design? How are these taken care of in the design?

It is not only in negotiation or in conflict that values matter. With any change whatsoever the values of those who are going to carry out the change and the values of those affected by the change are important. Then there are the values of the organization: time, cost, disruption, image, etc.

Excellent abstract designs which do not take values into account remain unusable.

Values are not fixed absolutes. Values can be added to. Values can be changed. There can be a trade-off in values where one value is given up in favour of another. Values can be enhanced.

Values are not always obvious. Sometimes even the person for whom a value applies is not aware of that value, because it is hidden or taken for granted. 'Freedom from fear' is seen as a value only when it is threatened.

In the end, concepts are only ways of delivering 'value'. So value is at the heart of the design process. But, just as the enjoyment of a meal is the ultimate test of the value of the 'meal outcome', so the effectiveness of the thinking process depends on the values provided at the end. The meal requires a lot of preparation, including assembling and preparing the ingredients and then cooking them. In the same way the design process may be complicated in order to deliver simple values at the end.

There are several broad strategies of design.

1. Look to the desired or ideal outcome and work backwards.
2. Design around the dominant theme or value and fit the others in.
3. Try to combine the different needs and values and see what the result looks like. Improve and modify as required.
4. Move ahead with a tentative design and allow the pressures of evolution to improve it.
5. Produce alternative designs and then compare them to each other and to the needs.
6. Select and borrow a standard design. Modify as required.
7. Identify the key point, design to fit that and then build the rest of the design around this point.
8. Simplify and strip the requirements to the bare essentials and deal only with these. Elaborate later.
9. Play around and try out different arrangements in an almost arbitrary fashion. Wait for some design to emerge.
10. Produce any design and then respond to criticism of this design by changing it as required.

There are many more strategies. There is no one right strategy. Different situations and different styles will make one or other seem more appropriate on any one occasion.

I have left until this point the business of checking the validity of a possibility. This is because the role of that possibility in the final design will determine how thoroughly it needs to be checked. If the possibility is central to the design then the checking has to be thorough. This is the same as for checking a hypothesis or any other type of possibility. We devise a way of checking it just as we might design an experiment. So at this point we do make a strong effort to see whether some possibility is valid. If we are unable to complete this checking process then our design has to incorporate the two possibilities: that the point is valid; that the point is not valid. The design should not depend on the validity of a point which has not been checked – unless we need to take action and are prepared to take a known risk about this.

Let us consider some parallels in the area of employment:

Big companies and governments are shedding people in the search for efficiency.

Modern technology means that fewer people are needed in production.

Many items can be made in countries with lower costs and lower social welfare and then be imported.

Competition seeks out the lowest-cost production.

Some people registered as unemployed are working in the black economy.

There are not enough jobs to go round.

Some people are not qualified for today's jobs.

Some people have got used to not working.

The change from unemployment to work may be too small to act as a motivator.

Income transfer through tax and welfare is inefficient.

As for values, we can find:

> The value of work to the worker.
> The value of work to society in providing goods or services.
> The value of goods and services to the consumer.
> The value of lower taxes if welfare costs are lower.
> The value of lower unemployment to the government in terms of costs and votes.

There are other values involved.

As for concepts, we can find:

> Fewer jobs available, due to the search for efficiency, competitive pressures, technology and low-cost imports. Weakness of income-transfer mechanisms through taxes and unemployment benefits.

Again, many other concepts could be extracted.

The designed outcome could include a range of options:

1. Methods for sharing existing jobs, with more leisure, etc. (early retirement, shared jobs, part-time, cafeteria-style, etc.).
2. Methods for creating new jobs that provide real value for society, and new ways of paying for these non-commercial jobs.
3. Limiting job loss through protectionism.
4. Job creation through support of small businesses.
5. Accepting some unemployment as a fact of life and a way of life.

The most interesting option of creating new jobs and finding non-commercial ways of paying for them sets another thinking task. The whole process of parallel thinking would then start again. Creativity would now play a large part both in contributing possibilities and then in designing forward from the field of possibilities. In the course of such a creative exercise we might put forward such concepts as 'work design' as a new profession and 'separate economic loops with their own currency'. The point is that the way forward does not have to be contained within the present situation. We need not proceed only from analysis to problem-solving. The whole generative part of thinking should be allowed to make its contribution. We are not simply 'searching for the truth' but designing possible ways forward.

The design process does not only include the design of outcomes from the field of parallel possibilities. As I indicated, we may design alternatives as possible outcomes. We may need to design priorities and ways of choosing between the alternatives. We may need to design ways of testing our choices.

The final step of the design process is to ask: 'What does this lead to?' We look to see what the outcome of the whole parallel-thinking process leads towards. It may be a better understanding of the situation. It may be a solution to a problem. It may be a way of achieving an objective. It may be a 'design' for something. It may be the resolution of a conflict or an agreement in a negotiation. Or the thinking process may have defined new areas for further thinking. Sometimes we may be unable to offer a satisfactory designed outcome. At other times an outcome may be offered but is known to be far from perfect.

What I want to emphasize is that in parallel thinking the focus is on the design process and not on the power politics of adversarial argument or on the analysis/judgement search for the truth. It is not a matter of 'finding' the solution but of 'designing the way forward'.

31 WISDOM VS. CLEVERNESS

Do you have to be ancient with a long white beard before you can be wise?

Can wisdom be taught, or does it arise from the accumulated experience of many years?

What do we mean by wisdom?

Traditionally, Western thinking has concentrated on cleverness rather than wisdom. What irritated the Athenians (some of them) about Socrates was that he was a 'clever' fellow. Whatever you said, Socrates would find a way to challenge and to refute it. Some of this refutation was clever wordplay and some was based on fallacious reasoning. Some was sound. There was no doubt, however, that Socrates was a clever fellow. He was trained as a sophist, which had something to do with this, because the sophists prided themselves on cleverness and taught cleverness in argument as a way of exerting power.

Socrates thought of himself as 'wise' because the oracle at Delphi had told him 'that no man was wiser than Socrates'. He reckoned that this wisdom lay in recognizing his own ignorance. He then proceeded to reduce this ignorance through a method of 'cleverness'.

Cleverness is like a sharp-focus lens. Wisdom is like a wide-angle lens.

Western thinking has been much concerned with puzzles, problem-solving and the search for the truth. The puzzles may range from complex self-generated philosophical conundrums to scientific investigation. In other areas there are 'problems to be solved'. In North American psychology all thinking is termed 'problem-solving', which reflects the action orientation of a pioneer country. There has to be an 'answer'. We have to get to the 'answer'. It could be claimed, with some justification, that this concern with cleverness has produced the scientific and technological progress of the West (even though this did not arise directly from the traditional thinking system).

Puzzles are there to be 'solved'. A picture is there to be enjoyed. Because of this cleverness/puzzle focus of Western thinking, we always want a definite outcome from our thinking. 'What is the solution?' 'What is the decision?' 'What is the truth?'

In the preceding section I described how the design process would work on a field of parallel possibilities in order to design a

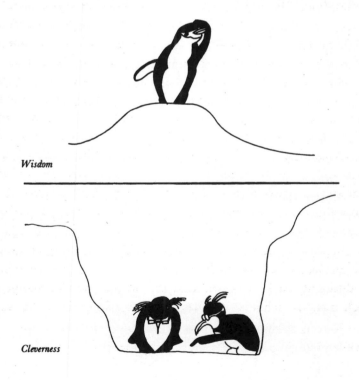

Wisdom

Cleverness

finite outcome. The intention would, indeed, be to get as finite an outcome as possible. This is fully in line with the normal intention of Western thinking. That is as it should be, because if parallel thinking is being put forward as an alternative to the Socratic method then parallel thinking must also be able to produce a finite outcome.

The advantage of parallel thinking, however, is that it is not restricted to 'cleverness'. Parallel thinking also works towards 'wisdom'.

Wisdom is a way of thinking, not just an accumulation of experience.

Most people suppose that if you set out with the formal techniques of lateral thinking to generate a needed new idea then the value of your thinking is determined by the values of the ideas generated in such a creative thinking session. In fact, the value of the creative thinking session goes far beyond this. In addition to the specific new ideas generated there is a range of new concepts, new possibilities, new approaches and new beginnings of ideas that have been brought into being in your mind during that creative session. Even if these are not immediately useful, they greatly expand your 'creative experience' around that subject. Your 'local wisdom' is greatly increased. Whenever you come to consider that subject again there is a greater repertoire of concepts and possibilities. Your 'mental garden' is better stocked with plants.

Part of wisdom is having a richer mental stock of possibilities, models, metaphors, concepts and ways of looking at things. Because of this richer stock of 'patterns', you can see the world in different ways. It is true that the normal way of acquiring such mental 'richness' is through living a long time. But such richness can be acquired much more quickly through deliberate creative effort.

Just as creative thinking develops a 'local wisdom' around some subject, so the field of parallel possibilities helps directly to develop wisdom. Instead of proceeding step by step, as in traditional thinking, there is, from the beginning, a broad view of the whole situation. Because there is no gatekeeper judgement of true/false, the field of possibilities can be large. Every possibility provides a 'hypothesis' through which to look at the world. As with science, that hypothesis may eventually be found to be useful or less useful, but the value of the hypothesis is as a way of 'seeing'.

So parallel thinking can also have the valuable output of a broader vision of the subject even when no finite outcome is intended or reached.

Many of the Socratic dialogues ended in failure because Socrates could refute all suggested 'definitions' that were offered to him. It was claimed that the discussion was nevertheless useful because a lot of ground had been covered in intelligent discussion. But a succession of refutations merely destroys 'weeds' but does not grow anything. In parallel thinking, the growing of possibilities does enrich the field of consideration.

Similarly the Socratic method of a series of guiding questions to lead the listener to the hoped-for answer is said to be a good teaching method. I am not sure that it is. The listener has simply done what he or she has been told, subtly, to do. Frameworks for genuine exploration of the subject by the student are possibly much more effective.

Can wisdom be taught? I believe that it can. The perception-broadening tools of the *CoRT Thinking Lessons** work towards this. If you always consider the purpose of your thinking, the factors involved, the people involved, your priorities and a range of alternatives, then you are going to be a great deal wiser than if you do not. If the thinking tools of the CoRT method become

* See page 84.

attention-directing habits then there is the 'operation' of wisdom which will itself accumulate experience and make good use of it. In practice the wisdom of even young children using the CoRT method is astonishing to observe. The concepts produced are not only fresh but also very relevant. It becomes obvious that wisdom is a way of thinking, not just an accumulation of experience.

Wisdom looks around broadly, and into the future beyond the immediate consequences. Wisdom is concerned with context and with circumstances. Wisdom looks at interconnections and interplay. Wisdom looks at possibilities and alternatives. Wisdom holds different possibilities in mind and has no need to choose one and to throw out the others. Wisdom considers the behaviour of non-linear systems instead of forcing everything into the linear model. Wisdom involves doubts and guesses and some risk-taking. Wisdom does not set out to 'prove' things but to follow possibilities. Wisdom is pragmatic, not authoritarian.

Japanese business has a much longer-term perspective than American business. This is partly because the short-term demands of the quarterly stock reports needed by the American stock exchanges are absent. Shareholders in Japan exert much less pressure than in America. But part of this longer-term perspective is the 'wisdom' of a broader picture. There is less emphasis on being 'smart' and making a fast buck.

When it comes to wisdom, Eastern thinking has tended to put more emphasis on this than has been the case in the West. This has meant an understanding and an acceptance of the world. There has been a willingness to adapt to the world rather than to change the world. Sometimes this has taken the form of 'changing yourself' rather than the world around. All this is different from the 'activism' of Western thinking, which sets out to wrest the truth from the world and then to use that to change the world.

There does not, however, have to be an either/or dichotomy. We do not have to choose between cleverness or wisdom. There are times when we need cleverness and there are times when we need wisdom. My point is that the very nature of Western thinking with its analysis, judgement, boxes and truth search has pushed us, inevitably, towards cleverness and away from wisdom.

Parallel thinking, with its generation of possibilities, its overlaps and its emphasis on 'what can be', provides a way of getting back to wisdom.

32 DIALECTIC VS. PARALLELS

Talking is fun and enjoyable. But how important is talking for thinking?

We know that language is both a great help and a great hindrance to thinking. It is a help because it allows us to hold on to and to manipulate complex matters. It is a help because it allows us to create concepts which do not exist in the outer world. It is a help because it allows us to operate the circular basis of perceptual truth. Language is a hindrance when it forces us to see things in particular ways. Language is a hindrance when a word comes with a lot of baggage and emotional shading (as with the word 'fascist'). It is a hindrance when it permits false analogies and either/or strategies. I have dealt with some of these aspects elsewhere.*

Dialectic is supposed to be the essence of the Socratic method. In Plato's brilliant fiction, Socrates is always involved in a dialectical discussion with various others. It is this interplay in terms of questions, answers, agreements and disagreements that is supposed to be the process which is going to lead to the 'true definitions' that Socrates sought. At times, however, Socrates might just as well have been preaching. He would make statements and then put them as questions, seeking agreement: 'Is this not so?'. I have covered that point in a previous section. The point

* See my book *I am Right, You are Wrong*.

I want to cover here is whether conversational interchange is so important for thinking as Socrates, and others, believed.

Thinking on your own is boring and requires a lot of self-discipline. Conversation is fun and it is lively. Someone may be able to think of something which is new to you. Someone else's remark may trigger new ideas. But you have to be more careful of what you say, because it could be challenged. We might summarize some of the aspects as:

1. Stimulation.
2. Additional ideas.
3. Challenge and attack.
4. Examples.
5. Suggestions.

All these aspects arise from the nature of the Western thinking tradition.

Because the production of ideas and possibilities is weak in traditional thinking, we need other people to put forward the possibilities. Otherwise they are not going to appear. This is similar to brainstorming, where you need many people to produce many ideas if you do not have the deliberate creative tools of lateral thinking.

Because 'truth' is partly going to be reached by rejecting 'untruth', there is a need for the 'untruth' to be seen to be rejected. The better the untruth is defended, the more valuable its rejection.

There is a need to lead someone step by step through a logical process in order to show how a conclusion has been reached.

Even genuine exploratory discussions can be considerably speeded up by using the frames of parallel thinking.

Strictly speaking, in parallel thinking there is no need for anyone else to be around. There is no need for questions to direct your attention, because there are specific attention-directing frames (as in the Six Hats method and also in CoRT). A subject can be thoroughly explored by a thinker entirely on his or her own. You direct your own attention.

With regard to additional ideas, additional suggestions and additional examples, these can be generated deliberately using the formal techniques of lateral thinking. Formal creative thinking does not need a group.

With regard to refutation and lawyer-type argument, this is not part of parallel thinking anyway.

How can a suggestion be thoroughly examined unless there are those who defend the idea and those who attack it? This point has been covered in a previous section. The simple answer is that a frame like the Six Hats encourages the same thinker to explore both the benefits of the idea and also the dangers.

Because there is no 'need' to have other people around when using parallel thinking does not mean that there is no merit in having people around. It is more fun to think in groups. Less self-discipline is required. People do provide additional parallel possibilities. Someone else's remark may trigger an idea of your own. My preference is for group meetings which alternate between individual thinking and group interaction.

What surprises most people who actually watch a parallel-thinking session is that the session is so lively and so motivated. Those who have been brought up to believe that interest comes only from 'clash' are surprised to find that the generation of parallel possibilities can be even more motivating because the hostile element is missing. Good contributions are acknowledged. There is the pleasure of insight when you suddenly see something a different way. There is also the pleasure of discovering something obvious which had not been noticed before. Structured exploration is, in fact, very motivating, because the mind goes through a series of 'mini-eurekas'. There is also the pleasure of seeing yourself use your mind thoroughly and effectively.

So there are benefits to be obtained by thinking in parallel in groups, but the dialectic process is not essential to parallel thinking.

It should also be mentioned that the conventional dialectic method is very time-consuming. Imagine you had to identify an apple by rejecting all 'non-apples'.

'This is not a pear.'

'This is not a banana.'

'This is not a tangerine.'

'This is not a plum', etc.

This is clearly an exaggeration, but dialectic does sometimes go rather like that. With parallel thinking we might say: 'There is a possibility this could be an apple. Where does that take us?' We do not even have to check the 'apple' hypothesis before we proceed to see 'what happens next'.

Groupware is a computer-based system in which people in a meeting put in their ideas 'in parallel' without dialectic. Not surprisingly, the process speeds up the meeting very considerably.

Not every discussion is an argument, but even genuine exploratory discussions can be considerably speeded up by using the frames of parallel thinking. It is amazing how much non-productive to and fro there is even in goal-oriented discussions.

So parallel thinking does not depend on dialectic as does the Socratic method. Nevertheless, there can be benefits in carrying out the parallel thinking in groups.

33 ACTION VS. DESCRIPTION

What is unique about action is that it always takes place in the future. That future may be the next second or two as you decide how to deal with a mugger or it may be the next 20 years as you plan an electric power-generating plant. Is marriage a 'description' of being in love or an action plan for the next 40 years?

Description takes place in the past. It may be the remote past and what the Aboriginals did in Australia 40,000 years ago or it may be the taste of the New Zealand Sauvignon Blanc wine that you have just sipped. You can seek to describe the future with extrapolations, scenarios, forecasts, prophecy and guessing. The doctor, in his or her mind, can project the course of a disease if it is not treated. But any 'description' of the future depends on an expectation that things will be the same as they have been in the past – either directly or through a combination of known effects.

When we describe the past there can be 'truth'. Witnesses and video cameras can describe what happened in a traffic accident. There may be accurate descriptions and less accurate descriptions. But if your son tends to drive your new car too fast you can only speculate as to what might happen. You can refer to statistics regarding the likelihood of accidents with young drivers who drive too fast, but those will only provide a probability. The statistics are 'true' because they are about the past. The application of them to an individual in the future is only a possibility with a probability.

Western culture has tended to make a sharp distinction between thinkers and doers. This is because the thinkers were dealing with truth and theology and science and the doers were merely mucking about and getting things done. For intellectuals, description is more satisfying than action because description deals with the 'truth'. What is there cannot change or escape from you. Examining a dead butterfly is a good deal easier than examining a flying butterfly. You can argue and debate about 'what is' but only trade speculations about 'what may be' as a result of a certain action. You can seek more information about the past, as in historical research. It is impossible to find accurate information about the future, except in predicting the continuity of certain events like the appearance of comets at defined times.

Because action is set in the future there is always a 'risk' element. Things might not go as planned. An unforeseen change in circumstances might produce a contrary result. When dealing with non-linear systems the result may indeed be uncertain. The reaction to the proposed action might be greater than expected, as with proposals for new taxes. Traditional Western thinking does not like the uncertainty of risk. If you have judgement with a true/false outcome then how do you deal with risk? To deal with risk you need the possibility/design aspects of parallel thinking.

If you believe that action springs directly from 'what is' then you are not concerned with the design of action. If you believe that 'what can be' has to be designed then you apply the design process to action itself.

Socrates believed and often stated that 'knowledge is virtue'. He believed that men acted incorrectly only out of ignorance.

The underlying assumption is that if you have an accurate and detailed street map then you will never lose your way (provided you have good eyesight and the ability to read maps). Once the street map is there then action is very simple: go straight ahead, turn right or turn left. So full knowledge will indicate to people what they 'should' strive to do and what they should strive to avoid. The details of the action are as unimportant as the details of walking down the street.

The success of science has reinforced the view that knowledge is enough. Putting the knowledge to work through technology is relatively simple. In any case, that technology becomes 'engineering' and we can put together knowledge about engineering and learn that also as knowledge.

We can lay down 'routine' actions. You can learn these routines just as an actress learns her lines in a play. When the right cue is given then the right speech is made – and in this way the play proceeds.

So knowledge is going to identify the situation, helped by the decision of 'judgement'. Once judgement has declared that it is indeed a particular situation then knowledge of the routine response will take care of the appropriate action. It can all be done with knowledge, just as a student will answer questions in an examination with material he or she has learned by rote.

Occasionally the situation may be more complex and we will have to analyse it before applying judgement. We analyse the complex situation into parts which are easier to identify. Then the routine action is applied. Before the days of modern medicine there used to be a joke about skin doctors. It was said that dermatology was simple: if the sore was wet you applied a powder; if the sore was dry you applied a cream. What was in the powder or cream did not much matter.

Sometimes it may be necessary to put together some routine segments of action. Sometimes it may be necessary to pause to reassess the situation and then apply the routine action.

Routine actions are either obvious (seek out, avoid) or they will have evolved over time. The technical skill of a craftsman has evolved over time and will be learned by daily experience as an apprentice to a master craftsman. Action skills are to be learned by apprenticeship. You learn to play music by playing music, not by reading about music.

To this day we believe very much the same things about action. There is routine action, and we can learn both the routines and when to apply them. Then there is 'on-the-job' learning, where experience gradually shapes required action patterns.

A group of developers may set out, at different times, with the same ability and drive, with the same capital and action skills. Some of them will become very successful and others will fail. We applaud (in some countries) the successful ones and ignore or laugh at the failures. Timing, luck and circumstances have sorted them out. Action of this sort is seen to be a 'hit-and-miss' affair.

So on the one hand we have routine action and on the other hand we have 'hit-and-miss' entrepreneurship. Where is the need to think about action?

Once again we come back to the fundamental difference between traditional Western thinking and parallel thinking. This is the difference between 'what is', which is concerned with description and truth, and 'what can be', which is concerned with possibility, design and action. If you believe, as the Socratic method does, that action springs directly from 'what is' then you are not concerned with the design of action. If you believe that 'what can be' has to be designed forward from a field of parallel possibilities then you apply the design process to action itself.

Because of the uncertainties involved, you cannot, or should not, attempt to design an action using the stepwise adversarial argument system in which you have to be 'right' at each step. Yet people try to do this every day in the business world. Traditional Western thinking is simply very inappropriate when applied to the design of action. Yet we have never sought to develop any other type of thinking, because we have been so complacent with our thinking habits, derived from the Gang of Three.

To deal with the future we have to deal with 'possibilities'. Analysis will only tell us 'what is'.

It is only in the military and in business that attention has been given to action thinking. It was the Prussian military philosopher Clausewitz who laid the basis for much of the subsequent work. Even so, much of the thinking is still based on the traditional thinking method of classify, identify and apply routine behaviour.

You can design a meticulous action plan with every step in place. You design in checkpoints and contingency rerouting should things turn out differently from what has been expected. That is one style.

You can forge ahead with some general objective and general guiding principles and then react to what you come across moment to moment, as a rock climber might do on a new face.

You can set sub-objectives and design action to achieve each of these in turn.

You can start with a routine type of action but with a great readiness to adapt and change this as you go along.

At one end of the action spectrum there is 'plan' and at the other end there is 'react'. Design comes in at all points. Plans have to be designed. Reaction has to be designed. You have to be in a suitable state to react; you have to pre-design reaction possibilities; you have to conceive in advance values and opportunities which will determine appropriate action. Reaction usually needs to be more sophisticated than 'run away' or 'gobble it up'. Your moment-to-moment reaction also requires 'thinking'. It is only too easy to assume that action is instinctive.

When IBM was founded, the company made weighing scales. So it was quite an achievement for Thomas J. Watson

Sr. President of the organization, to have insisted on the motto 'THINK'. IBM did think, and became very successful. Then, like most successful companies, it got trapped in its own culture. It wanted to maximize success. That means dealing with 'what is' rather than 'what can be'.

To deal with the future we have to deal with 'possibilities'. Analysis will only tell us 'what is', which is why business schools are not turning out the best business thinkers. IBM's analysis revealed that it totally dominated the market in mainframe computers, and these were high-profit items. Attention to 'possibilities' would have revealed that mainframes might be threatened by local area networks and distributed processing. Attention to possibilities might have suggested emerging competitors as the technology of computers became more of a 'commodity'. It is likely that such considerations were raised somewhere in IBM but it proved difficult to design these into action when day-to-day success suggested providing only more of the same.

In the short-term thinking of American business, today's profits are certainties. If you do not look after them you may not be around to enjoy tomorrow's possibilities. That makes the design of action difficult, because it tends to be a description of 'what is'.

A dancer learns the routine ballet steps, which are limited in number. Then the choreographer puts these steps together as an action sequence. Finally it is the artistic talent of the dancer that puts the steps together in the choreographed sequence but with spirit, passion and expression. The choreographer has the design task, but the technology of the steps has to be there and final effectiveness depends on the talent of the performer.

Traditional thinking has simply not been action-oriented. The static judgement/box habits of traditional thinking can deal only with the past and with stable situations. For dealing with changing situations the methods, attitudes and processes of parallel thinking are possibly more appropriate. There is a need to work forwards from a field of parallel possibilities in order to 'design' action.

34 VALUE VS. TRUTH

So dominated have we become by the belief system of the Gang of Three that any mention of 'truth' causes a shudder of horror. There is horror that we might abandon truth for expediency or utilitarianism. There is horror that we might abandon sacrosanct principles (which in practice we do all the time) for relativism. There is horror that pragmatism might replace absolute truth and so put society at the mercy of political profiteers. No matter how little our action may reflect that belief, we like to believe in 'truth'. Just as having a monarch in Great Britain prevents the emergence of a political president, so having 'truth' up there prevents the emergence of some 'dangerous' replacement.

Once again it is important to remember the immediate background to the thinking of Socrates/Plato. Because we cannot really distinguish what was Socrates from what Plato made Socrates say in Plato's work, we sometimes need to consider the Socrates/Plato combination. The immediate intellectual background consisted of the 'foreign' (born in Greek cities other than Athens) sophists, who demanded fees for teaching students rhetoric or the art of persuasion. These people (or most of them) believed that truth was relative, that perception established a personal 'truth' for everyone and that 'expediency' was all that mattered. Such basic beliefs meant that you could change someone's 'truth' through persuasion, and the skills of persuasion were therefore very powerful because they could become the source of power in a society where persuasion in both politics and business was all-important. I do not want to try to distinguish here between those sophists who were really ultra-modern in their thinking and those who were opportunistic charlatans. There is the same problem with management 'sophists' today.

What matters is that Socrates/Plato set out to put truth on an absolute, unchanging and non-subjective basis. They succeeded very well indeed. Aristotle then came along and gave order and substance to this system. In that way the Gang of Three determined our thinking about 'truth'.

'Truth', 'valid' and 'value' all overlap a great deal. Philosophers love to attack this overlap and to put each into its proper box. It is not my intention to do this here.

If you were to make nails of gold, would they have a value? You could sell them for the gold content. You could store them as a hedge against inflation. You might even make a super-luxury gift box held together by gold nails. You would, of course, have to drill small holes for the nails to pass through, because the softness of gold would make it impossible to use the nails in the usual way. Yet 'gold' is a valuable metal. Surely the value of gold is intrinsic to the metal?

We do not merely seek to discover which value should prevail. We seek to reconcile values where possible. We seek to design ways in which values can come to change.

If you made a gun barrel out of gold it might not be much use. But why would you want a gun anyway? If you want a gun to attack people, that may be a value to you but not to society. If you want a gun to go fight to defend your country against invaders then society welcomes that value even if it is rather dangerous to you personally.

Aspirin is a dangerous compound, because many people kill themselves with an overdose of aspirin. Prolonged, heavy use of aspirin may cause gastrointestinal bleeding. In rare cases young children can have a violent reaction to aspirin. So is aspirin bad? Not at all – it is the most used of compounds. When you have a severe headache there is nothing more wonderful than the power of aspirin to remove that headache. Some people find that aspirin relieves the pain of their arthritis. There is good evidence that half an aspirin a day may reduce the incidence of heart attacks in middle-aged men. So how can something be good and bad at the same time?

This was exactly the sort of argument that Protagoras made. Anyone concerned with medicine comes across the relativity of value – relativity with regard to amount, relativity with regard to diagnosis, relativity with regard to stage of an illness, relativity with regard to individual reactions. So how do we deal with the 'truth' about aspirin being 'good'? The 'truth' is that aspirin can be both good and bad. The trouble is only with our 'box'. You need to specify the situation in order to determine whether aspirin is 'good' or 'bad'.

It is much simpler to consider 'value'. Value is directly to do with 'relationships'. Value is relative. A thump on the head with an ingot of gold could be very dangerous.

The fault of Western thinking has been to pay insufficient direct attention to value. This has been because of the possible confusion between 'truth' and value (as in the minds of the sophists) and the danger of regarding 'truth' as relative. The second reason for this neglect was the one we have come across so often before: the belief that from 'truth' will spring everything else.

Every stone has value in an arch, because it serves the function of that system. Yeast and the control of temperature have value in fermentation, because they serve that system's function. Values force us to think of systems.

The system of a small chemical plant gives value to cost reduction, because this leads to profit. Profit has value for the owner, or shareholders, of the plant and also for the workers, because they have jobs. The workers having jobs is of value to their families, who need feeding. But the effluent from the plant may be polluting the river. This has a negative value for the wildlife in the river, for people downstream, for the general level of pollution in the world, for attitudes to pollution, for pollution-conscious crusaders, etc.

Because multiple systems can coexist, side by side or one within another, so values also coexist. We can then think about some values being higher than others or we can argue about which values should prevail. Traditional thinking on the lines of 'I am right, you are wrong' seeks to sort out these value conflicts by arguing that one set of values is 'right' and the other set 'wrong'. Obviously, there will be different opinions on this depending on which system you are in. Should the developing countries hold up their development because the developed countries have done their development and done their polluting and are now more concerned about a pollution-free world? Can the world afford more pollution whatever the rights and wrongs of the situation?

The judgement/box system of traditional thinking does not work with such a problem. Lawyer-type adversarial argument does not work unless there is a new code of environmental laws to which everyone subscribes. We have to use parallel thinking and design.

A good example of 'design' is the concept of 'tradeable pollution permits'. A factory that is currently polluting obtains a 'permit to pollute'. Immediately that sounds awful and totally contrary to what we want. Judgement would usually reject such an idea – unless the whole-system picture was taken into account. If that factory cleans up its effluent then that permit can be sold to another factory. So there is now 'cash value' in cleaning up the pollution. There is also another, more hidden, value: time is given to the factory to clean up its effluent. I am not suggesting that this is the only way to do things, or even the best way, but I am suggesting that this is a good example of a 'designed way forward'.

Where there are conflicting values it is somewhat pointless to seek to argue which are the superior values or which are 'right' and which 'wrong'. I am not suggesting that all values are equal or that there is no such thing as a 'wrong' value. The showing of excessive violence on television clearly has a value in terms of audience rating, advertising rates and job success of the programme directors involved. But the effect on society is the negative value of lowering the acceptance threshold for violence. I am not sure that this is any different from any form of exploitation in which the value of the exploiter is different from the values of the exploited. An extra value is, however, pulled in. This is the value of 'freedom of expression'. There is the suggested fear that censorship of violence on television could be the 'thin end of the wedge' and that censorship would soon extend to political choices and other values (just as Plato wished). A 'designed' way around this difficulty would be to allow violence but to put a price on it. There might be a cost of £10,000 for every murder each time the show was aired. There would be a scale of prices for other forms of violence. There would now be a cost consideration. If we must have that murder 'for its dramatic necessity' then there is a cost, just as there would be a cost if you 'had to' shoot the film in Tahiti. Considerations of production and showing cost would now apply. Yet you could still show what you wanted. The money would go to victims of violence.

What I am seeking to show is that 'design' is not 'discovery'. We do not merely seek to discover which value should prevail. We seek to reconcile values where possible. We seek to design ways in which values can come to change. We seek to design ways in which people can be free to choose values. People should be free to smoke if they know what they are doing, are prepared to pay their full healthcare costs (if necessary) and do not impose their smoking on others.

Values are determined by systems, contexts and circumstances.

In practice we seek to operate a pragmatic hierarchy of values: the planet, the general good, society, the community, the family and one's self. Sometimes we take refuge in custom or tradition. Sometimes we take refuge in majority voting or opinion polls. Almost always we would like to argue from 'basic moral principles' or the law. We feel most comfortable with that, because we are then on the solid ground of right/wrong. That others might have a different view of right/wrong as it applies to values is as irrelevant here as it is in any other situation. My 'right' is based on truth – yours is not.

There are times when a decision about values or a choice of values does have to be based on the absolutes of some belief system. There is no need to exclude or deny that. Parallel thinking does not have to operate with 'never' or 'always'. The point is that if we develop the 'design' habits of parallel thinking then we may be able to cope with many conflicts of value better than we are able to at the moment using our traditional thinking system.

Is this just a plea for 'relativity' and 'pragmatism'? Those are judgement boxes with habitual values attached to them. Many values are relative whether we like it or not. Why not 'all' values? Because there is no need to make that claim. Pragmatism implies a choice of what is most 'useful' under the circumstances. Pragmatism is still based on 'what is': the choice is between existing options. Parallel thinking puts the emphasis on design and on the creation of new options. Into this design process can go fundamental principles and 'absolute' values. These are not excluded. Many people find that an 'absolute' prohibition of killing another person is somehow overcome by the context of war or self-defence. True pacifists and true vegetarians are rare.

One of the difficulties with traditional thinking is the gate-keeper judgement system in which each statement has to be judged before being accepted into the 'party'. Each contribution is challenged and has to prove itself. You cannot make a chain if some of the links are defective. However, particularly with values, but also with other matters, it is sometimes necessary to get the 'whole picture' before the contribution of each part can be assessed. It is similar to needing to know what aspirin is going to be used for before judging whether aspirin is good or bad. Is it a good move or a bad move to raise the price of some goods you are trying to sell? It depends on the economic situation at the time. It depends on the market and distribution system you are in. It depends on whether the goods can carry a prestige label. It depends on whether the price rise is sufficient to propel the goods into a different 'class'. It depends on how you use the extra profit from the higher margins (if the price rise is a matter of choice, not necessity). Is this extra money going to be used for promotion or for better packaging, or is it just going to give extra profits?

With parallel thinking all the possibilities are fed in and laid alongside each other. The picture may then become clear. Sometimes a decision can be made immediately; at other times there is a need to design a way forward. We may need to launch a new version of the product at a higher price rather than just putting the price up.

Values are determined by systems, contexts and circum-stances. They are also determined by perceptions. There is the story of a perfume which became successful only when the mar-keters quadrupled the price. Did people assume that if it was so expensive then it must be the best? Did people prefer the 'price judgement' to their own sense of smell? Did people find value in giving as a present the most expensive perfume possible? To some people such things smack of the trickery and deceit of advertisers and marketers who set out to persuade people with the same sort of trickery that was taught by the sophists, who also set out to change perceptions. But is this a fair assessment? If you want to indicate to someone that you are giving that person an expensive present because you value her and because she only deserves the best, is that not a genuine value? If you genuinely do not trust your own sense of smell, is it not reasonable to suppose that a perfume that can continue to sell at a high price must be good?

We feel that all these things are separate from the real intrinsic value of the perfume: the truth. But the whole business of perfume is about perception and image. Those are the systems that create the value. Maybe you want your friends to recognize that you are wearing an expensive perfume. In fact there are cheap generic perfumes which often are almost exactly the same as the expensive ones (which is permitted so long as they do not use the same name). You could really buy those, if you trusted your nose, and get almost the same effect – except for the present-giving value.

It is important to explore values which are not always obvious. It is also important to design values which are not there until you have designed them. The value of selling a half doughnut is that the buyer would feel 'virtuous' in not eating the other half. This is a different value from eating a small doughnut, where the 'uneaten' half is not perceptually present.

The value of gossip and rumour in society and in political matters has been consistently underestimated by political theorists. The value of such matters is that they themselves set values.

When a political party has been in power a long time and long enough to mess up the economy and other matters, that party has a good chance of being re-elected if the economy is bad enough. This is because the opposition is now seen as a bunch of amateurs with no experience of running a country in difficult times.

It is said that some couples 'enjoy' quarrelling, because it is stimulating, because it relieves boredom and because it still indicates passion for each other. Some people prefer to be hated rather than ignored. There are times when people do not really want their complaints attended to – they prefer to have the opportunity to grumble about something. Are such things true, occasionally true or cynical myths?

Value sensitivity and valufacture (a new word*) give value to life. Art is a value-producing exercise. Should art just reveal by highlighting and distilling values that are always there, or should art seek to open up new values? Belief systems are the ultimate creator and arbiter of the values that decide behaviour. Socrates believed that knowledge alone could do this – that was another belief system.

In dealing with values there is a need to consider parallel possibilities. That is why parallel thinking is important for exploring values, reconciling values and creating new values. Design is part of the process.

* See my book *Surpetition* (London: HarperCollins, 1992).

35 WATER LOGIC AND PARALLEL THINKING

What is the relationship between 'water logic' and parallel thinking? At various points in this book I have referred to water logic, and there may be some confusion about how it fits in with parallel thinking.

What is the relationship between spaghetti and tomato sauce?

What is the relationship between a pair of trousers and the zip?

Parallel thinking is the overall general method of thinking.

Water logic is a type of logic used in parallel thinking.

In traditional thinking, adversarial argument (dialectic) is a general method. Within the argument there is the use of 'is/is not' logic, induction, deduction and other ways of handling ideas.

You could use parallel thinking without using water logic just as you can eat spaghetti without tomato sauce or wear trousers without a zip. But for various reasons, which I shall go into below, something like water logic is both useful and needed in parallel thinking.

Traditional logic is based on 'is' and 'definitions'. The definitions are what we seek, and that is what Socrates was all about. Once we have the definition then we 'judge' whether something fits that definition or not.

Water logic is based on 'to' and 'destinations'. 'What does this lead to?' 'What comes next?' It is more like a road where each town on the road leads to the next town.

Water logic is the logic of perception and self-organizing information systems. Traditional logic is a 'game' we play with the external world, using language boxes as definitions. It is the logic of systems which require an external organizer rather than being self-organizing.

In parallel thinking there is a strong place for creativity. Parallel thinking is not just about judging (critical thinking) but about generating possibilities. Creativity is one of the ways of generating possibilities.

Creativity is more than just sitting and waiting for new ideas. We can use the deliberate and formal techniques of lateral thinking to generate ideas. One of these techniques involves 'provocation'. In provocation we put forward a statement which is not part of our experience. For example, we might say: 'Po a cinema ticket should cost $100.' Obviously there is no point in 'judging' that provocation as such. Instead of the mental operation of 'judgement' we use the mental operation of 'movement', so we move forward to the idea of providing cinema-goers with a simple way of investing in a film they have just seen. This is an idea I once presented to the Swedish film board, which was seeking new ideas for financing films. This moving forward is a clear example of water logic.

Parallel thinking is action-oriented. We move from possibilities to the direct design of action.

The first stage of parallel thinking is to do with laying down a field of parallel possibilities. Parallel thinking is concerned with 'possibilities' more than with the judgement of 'truth'. What are you going to do with a possibility? You move forward to see what it leads to. You move forward to see what it contributes. We use a hypothesis (possibility) in science to lead us to look at things in a certain way and to lead us to design experiments to get further data. With possibilities it is almost essential to use water logic. 'What happens next?'

In parallel thinking we do not need to use boxes with hard edges and the ruthless judgement that fits or forces things into these boxes. There is 'overlap'. Something can be both A and a bit of B at the same time. If we cannot fit things into the boxes, then what are we going to do? We move forward to see what happens. In traditional thinking we use contradictions to prove error and to force choices. In parallel thinking we embrace both possibilities and move forward to see what results.

In parallel thinking we can put together a group of things, or parallel possibilities, and then 'look to see what happens'. One of the techniques of lateral thinking is the 'stratal'.* Here we simply put down, in parallel, about five statements about the matter and then see what these lead to. The statements 'sensitize' patterns in the brain, and we look to see what follows. This is part of the dynamics of water logic rather than the static descriptive activity of rock logic.

Instead of the instant gatekeeper judgement of each part, parallel thinking seeks to build up an overall picture of the entire system. We look to see what each part contributes to the system. We first collect as many possibilities as possible and then look to see what each possibility contributes. 'What does this lead to?'

Whereas traditional thinking is description-oriented – on the basis that if you 'know what is' then action is easy – parallel thinking is action-oriented. 'What action does this lead to?' We seek to design action chains. We move from possibilities to the direct design of action. We do not have to apply judgement boxes first.

* My book *Serious Creativity*.

The emphasis in parallel thinking is on 'design' rather than on analysis. 'How do we "design forward" from the field of parallel possibilities?' 'How do possibilities lead into a design?' 'What would the proposed design, itself, lead to?' The emphasis is on 'What next?' We could borrow standard designs, but in all other cases the design does not exist until we put it together. An architect does not 'discover' houses but needs to 'design' them. This is the fundamental difference between the 'search' idiom of traditional Western thinking (prospecting for gold) and the 'design' idiom of parallel thinking (constructive).

A very specific use of water logic is in the flowscape technique.* Here, in a field of parallel possibilities, we look to see which other possibility follows from every item. The final flowscape gives us a picture of our perception of the matter. 'Where are the stable loops?' 'What is the "drainage" pattern?' 'Which points are highly sensitive and which points are peripheral?' We might also see how the flow patterns change if circumstances change. In this technique we see a simple example of how information can come to organize itself.

'What does a particular popic [suggested term for "possible picture of the world"] lead to?' 'What happens if we switch to another popic?' We can try things out. We can compare. All this is part of parallel thinking and different from judgement thinking.

Traditional Western thinking is firmly based on 'judgement'. Once we move away from judgement we come to the movement of water logic. 'Where does this take us?' 'What does this lead to?'

What we are seeking is the formation of perceptions, concepts, ideas and pictures of the world (popics). Once we have these then we can see their utility and check them out as required. There is a belief not that we shall discover the 'truth' but that information will come together to give us a 'possible'

* See my book *Water Logic*.

design for action or understanding. There is a belief that, given a chance, information may have a self-organizing tendency in the human brain – but not on a piece of paper.

There is an apparent overlap with the 'pragmatism' of William James. He was concerned with 'practical differences'. He wanted to get away from the elaborate word games of philosophers to ask what practical difference a particular statement made. He was interested in the 'truth value' of a statement, which he called the 'cash value'. There is a similarity inasmuch as parallel thinking is also concerned with the design of practical action. But parallel thinking is concerned with 'possibilities'. In that respect it is almost the opposite of the pragmatism of William James.

The emphasis in parallel thinking is on 'design' rather than on analysis.

If you put a number of interactive chemicals into the same solution then you expect something to happen. You expect compounds to form from the interactive elements. In the same way, if we feed parallel possibilities into our consideration we expect outcomes to form. We can help this with the 'design' process.

Ideas and statements are not fixed in their 'definition boxes' in parallel thinking. They are allowed to 'flow forwards' with water logic. We look to see 'what next' rather than 'what is'.

So we can see how the general idiom of water logic is very much part of parallel thinking. In addition there are times when the specific application of the 'movement' of water logic is used.

36 OVERLAP

A fundamental characteristic of parallel thinking is the avoidance of hard-edged judgement boxes. There is a preference for 'flagpoles' and for 'overlap' as suggested in Figure 18. There is no need to 'include' and to 'exclude'. There is no intellectual 'racism'. There is no need to use words like 'never', 'always', 'must', 'cannot', 'all' or 'none'. There are not the sharp dichotomies of true/false, right/wrong and either/or.

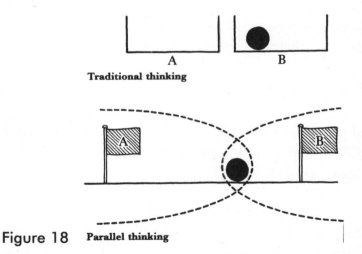

Traditional thinking

Figure 18   Parallel thinking

Readers will have observed that in writing this book I have, from time to time, used the traditional methods of thinking to point out the deficiencies of traditional thinking. Surely this proves the very utility of traditional thinking? Several points are involved here.

The first point arises from overlap. There is utility in traditional thinking, and I have made that point throughout the book. There are times when judgement and criticism are very useful. So when judgement is needed why should I not use the existing judgement system? There is no need to have an either/or situation. We do not have to throw out traditional thinking completely in order to use parallel thinking. My purpose in writing this book has been to point out the deficiencies of traditional thinking. It is inadequate for generating ideas. It is inadequate for designing outcomes. It is obsessed with judgement and judgement boxes. It believes that refutation is a way of getting to the truth. The emphasis is on 'search' rather than 'construction'. You can have clothes that are fine for a summer holiday in the Caribbean but totally inadequate for a Scandinavian winter. But the clothes are useful in their place. The folly is to assume that these clothes are sufficient for all occasions. It is this belief in the completeness of the traditional thinking system that has led to the failure of Western thinking where 'design' is needed.

The brain works directly with fuzzy overlap. Activity in one region sensitizes other regions. The excellence of the brain does not arise from its organization as a filing system of discrete pigeonholes, but from its organization as a system of multiple overlaps.

The second point is that I was brought up in the traditional thinking system, because parallel thinking had not yet been defined. So, from time to time, I slip back into that mode. The designer of a Grand Prix racing car is not necessarily the best driver of that car. In a similar way I may design thinking methods and tools but that does not mean that I am going to be the best user of these methods and tools. I would expect that youngsters who grow up with an understanding of parallel thinking will become much better at it than I am myself. This can be seen in schools where youngsters start using such methods as the Six Hats and the *CoRT Thinking Lessons*.

The third point is that most of the readers of this book will have been educated in the traditional thinking system, so it is necessary to 'talk that language'. If you go to France you are best understood if you talk French. In the same way, I fully expect that reviewers of this book will try very hard indeed to force the ideas expressed into specific judgement boxes, because that will be their method of working.

The chapters in this book are not separate watertight boxes. There is a great deal of overlap, and even repetition. That is necessary in order to build up the whole picture. Just as parallel possibilities can overlap as they contribute to the overall picture, so do the chapters in this book. The same thing can be said in different ways and in different places. What matters is the overall picture that is built up. It is only traditional thinking which insists on sharp definitions as a way of proceeding. If you want a 'possible' definition of parallel thinking it could be:

'The creation of a field of parallel possibilities from which to design a way forward.'

Is this the 'best' definition? No. It is just a possible definition.

It is this belief in the completeness of the traditional thinking system that has led to the failure of Western thinking where 'design' is needed.

We like hard-edged boxes because our thinking is essentially based on whether we agree that something goes into one box rather than another or whether we agree that the label on a box is correct.

We like to think in terms of 'us' and 'them'. We like to think of the 'goodies' and the 'baddies'. We like to think that something is 'wonderful' or 'awful'. We like to know whether we should eat what is put in front of us or reject it.

The overlap of parallel thinking permits phrases like:

'sort of ...'

'a bit of both ...'

'democracy-like systems ...'

'in the region of ...'

'related to ...'

'perhaps ...' 'maybe ...' 'possibly ...' 'could be ...'

To those brought up on the fixity and rigidity of traditional Western thinking such phrases are acutely irritating and uncomfortable. It is like looking up a number in a telephone book and finding that the print is too small to read.

Yet the brain works directly with fuzzy overlap. Activity in one region sensitizes other regions. Stimulation in a new region also has its areas which it sensitizes. Eventually an area that has been sensitized from different directions becomes activated itself, as in Figure 19. This is the exact process of overlap that is the basis of parallel thinking and parallel possibilities. The excellence of the brain does not arise from its organization as a

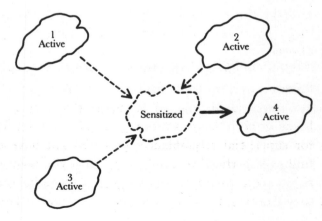

Figure 19

filing system of discrete pigeonholes, but from its organization as a system of multiple overlaps.

There is overlap between this book and several of my previous books. This book brings together ideas that have started elsewhere. In particular there is overlap with my book *I am Right, You are Wrong*. The difference is that in that book I related traditional thinking methods to the way the brain works as a self-organizing information system. At the end of that book readers may have been looking for the practicalities of an alternative system that uses 'water logic' rather than 'rock logic'. This current book provides that practical alternative. In this book I have set out the practical general thinking method of 'parallel thinking'. The emphasis has been directly on this method, both in itself and in contrast to traditional Western thinking.

There is overlap with other books such as *Serious Creativity* and *Water Logic*. I have referred to these books, but it has been quite impractical to go into the details of the specific thinking techniques put forward in those books. The same comment applies to the book *Six Thinking Hats* and to the *CoRT Thinking Lessons*, which contain specific procedures for applying parallel thinking.

I can never be sure that every reader of this book will have read previous books of mine, so I cannot take things for granted. On the other hand, those who have read previous books may find some of the points repeated. All this is part of the process of overlap.

You could claim that an apple is the 'same as' an orange because they are both 'fruit'. Being a little bit more specific, you might claim that an orange is the same as a tangerine because both have an orange-coloured skin. If you look for superficial resemblances you will not have difficulty in finding superficial resemblances. But if you want to enjoy the substance of an apple, an orange or a tangerine then you have to go deeper than superficial resemblances. To extract the maximum value you may have to become a gourmet who can even recognize the different tastes of oranges from different countries. It has never been difficult to be superficial.

When we look at the world around, there is a huge amount of overlap of our 'attention areas'. We do not have built into our eyes a sort of grid through the squares of which we proceed systematically. Sometimes we may look at the broad picture and sometimes at a detail. We get the complete picture from this overlap. That is exactly the purpose of overlap both in parallel thinking and in the writing of this book.

37 CHANGE VS. STABILITY

Should we change for the sake of change? The answer should be 'No', but there are good reasons for saying 'Sometimes'.

There are areas like art and fashion where change is the energizer. Without change, things get bogged down in sameness. Change gives excitement and stimulation. Change allows new directions to emerge.

There is complacency where we settle down within the game we have set for ourselves. A classic example is 'education', which sets its own criteria (usually remote from the needs of society) and then feels satisfied at fulfilling these.

There is no reason at all for supposing that the way we do something is the best way. The particular sequence of experiences that set up the current method need not have been optimal. If we are willing to make the effort we can often find new ways which are simpler, more effective and cost less.

So there can be good reasons to seek to change even when there is no strong necessity for change. But what about when there is a strong need to change?

The world around is changing. Technology is driving change. Populations are growing. Values are changing. Developing nations are developing faster. Pollution is increasing. People are living longer.

We can pretend that change is not happening or that it does not affect us or that we can insulate ourselves from change. We can seek to 'go back to basics' or to recreate the 'good old days'.

We can seek to resist change at all costs.

We can wait until the pressure for change is overwhelming and then, grudgingly, give way.

We can hope that the evolutionary pressures of change will gradually mould our existing ideas and values so that there need be no sudden or conscious change.

We find dealing with change particularly difficult, because traditional Western thinking (the Socratic method, the Gang of Three) was never designed for change. It was designed for a stable society in which there could be no concept of the very rapid changes of the last 100 years or so. Why should we suppose that three clever Greek philosophers sitting in the city state of ancient Athens would have devised a thinking system that would be capable of dealing with the rapid change we see around us?

Not only is this traditional thinking system poor at dealing with change, it can even be dangerously rigid. Socrates was searching for 'true definitions'. Plato was concerned with the 'absolute, unchanging ideal forms'. While we may still prefer that the principles governing human behaviour should remain unchanged, this belief in 'true unchanging concepts' should be severely restricted.

If we have a thinking system that is not intended to produce change, it is not surprising that we do not have much confidence in the change process.

There are fundamental concepts in society which may indeed need changing. These might include: money, economics, employment, work, education, democracy, justice, health, etc. We have come to regard all these as absolutes and unchangeables. Our design thinking still plays around with the existing concepts rather than designing new ones. We still hope that evolutionary pressures will teach us better ways of operating these traditional concepts. We cannot conceive that such fundamental concepts may need changing.

Change needs 'possibility' and 'design'. How can a judgement/box system be any good for change? Is it enough to sit and hope that ideas will somehow emerge and present themselves for judgement? Even if they do, will it be much use judging them in terms of the 'old' boxes?

The good is the enemy of the best. The adequate is the enemy of the better. Because our traditional concepts (including our thinking system) are more or less adequate, we see no great need to change them. At best we would accept an imperceptible 'drift' type of change, so that things become different without any sharp change-points.

We prefer the method of modification to produce change, because this is so much less risky than radical redesign. Yet in certain areas such as economics, and possibly democracy, radical redesign may be needed. Defending existing ideas is worthy and often very well done but is not, itself, a change process. Let others seek to change and we shall resist change. From this dialectic clash might come the sober change that is needed. But will it? That sort of change may be far too slow and also inadequate. In self-organizing systems, adjustment is usually not enough. If we play around with the same basic pieces we will get the same sort of outcomes. There comes a time when we need to challenge and rethink the 'pieces' themselves.

A fundamental defect in our traditional thinking system is the belief that evolution will throw up new ideas and that judgement will provide the harsh environment in which only the better ideas will survive. Very little technical progress would have been made if we had followed the same route in technology. We would still be working on improved paddle wheels on boats. In fact the only reason there was a change from the paddle wheel to the screw was that a test could be arranged. There was a tug of war and, to the horror of the Admiralty, the screw ship happily pulled the paddle wheeler backwards through the water. But how can we arrange similarly finite tests for concepts in other areas? How can we design the new ideas to be tested?

We can be creative about what we set out to achieve. We can be creative about how we achieve a traditional objective. We may design new values, or design to achieve existing values. In many fields we are able to assess good designs because they achieve what they are supposed to achieve. So there is no absolute reason why we should not be able to assess the worth of a new concept. We do this not by judging it in comparison to an old concept but in terms of what the new concept delivers.

Should we never try a new wine, because there is no absolute way of proving that it tastes better than the ones we know? There is risk, but there is also reward.

If we have a thinking system that is not intended to produce change, it is not surprising that we do not have much confidence in the change process. When we develop skill in parallel thinking, in possibilities, in creativity and in design, then we might be better able to cope with change. But how much effort are we putting into developing those skills? Very little – because we still believe that information, analysis and judgement are sufficient.

Gold is stable and unchanging, but its practical use is limited. Absolute truth is stable and unchanging, but its practical use is limited to making judgements and to providing the ingredients for the design process.

Potatoes do not make a meal until you learn how to cook them. By all means judge the taste of the cooked meal, but do not expect judgement to design the cooking method.

A fundamental defect in our traditional thinking system is the belief that evolution will throw up new ideas and that judgement will provide the harsh environment in which only the better ideas will survive.

We get caught in a vicious circle. The worse we are at designing better concepts then the more important it becomes for judgement to assess these concepts. But the more importance we give to judgement the less are we going to develop the design skills for producing better concepts. If you do not provide your children with behaviour models then discipline becomes necessary to control their behaviour, but discipline is itself a poor behaviour model.

That is why we should no longer continue to believe that the judgement aspects of traditional thinking are sufficient to cope with the changes that are needed. Defending existing ideas only appears an adequate way of coping with the need for change.

38 NEW LANGUAGE DEVICES

Do we need new language devices, or does existing language allow us to do all the things we want to do? Your existing cooking pots may allow you to cook all the meals you have always cooked, but if one day you want to cook dim sum then you may need to get a proper steamer system. Or you can decide that, since your existing pots are not designed for cooking dim sum, you should exclude the possibility of dim sum from your diet – after all, you have done pretty well without dim sum so far. Or you might put together some ad hoc system of strainers and saucepans to achieve the same effect as a proper steamer.

Similarly with language: we can regard as unnecessary and not worth doing those things which language does not permit or we can seek to achieve them in a clumsy ad hoc way and then claim that this is perfectly adequate.

I invented the word 'po' because there did not exist an adequate language device which allows us to signal that we are making a deliberate provocation. We know that provocation is mathematically necessary in any self-organizing system – and all the indications are that perception takes form in a self-organizing system. Therefore provocations are both necessary and useful. To be sure you can say: 'Listen, I am now going to put forward a provocation and I want you all to treat this as a provocation ... ' You could do this, but it is inconvenient.

We do not really need the question mark in punctuation, because the questioner could always say: 'What follows is intended to be a question, so treat it as a question.' The simple question mark is rather more convenient.

In order to carry out parallel thinking effectively, we need some language form that allows us to ask for 'parallels' and also to indicate that we are putting forward 'parallels'.

'Put a parallel ... '

'Place a parallel ...'

'Throw a parallel ...'

'Offer a parallel ...'

The very word 'parallel' also needs to come to exist in its own right, just as the word 'alternative' exists. The Gang of Three created their own vocabulary with 'ideal forms', 'essence', 'substance', etc. It is very often necessary to create a new word or to give a more specific meaning to an existing word in order to convey a new concept.

We do not have to be complacent about what existing language can do for us. There is no reason to suppose that language has reached a stage of perfection and cannot be changed for the better.

Just as we have a question mark in written language, so we can also have a symbol for parallels. This is suggested in Figure 20. The symbol is placed after a subject to imply a request for parallels. The symbol is placed before a statement to indicate that this is a parallel.

Figure 20 //

Examinations in education. //
// Continuous assessment.
// A way of motivating students to study.
// Making employment selection easier.
// Testing a student's exam-taking ability.
// Accountability of education.
// Satisfying parents.
// Quality control.
// Frequent oral assessment.

In practice there is no need to put the symbol before each parallel: it would be enough to put it at the beginning of the set of parallels.

In parallel thinking we often need to bring together a cluster of items, concepts, perceptions and possibilities in order to see 'what happens next'. This is very much part of water logic. The relationship between the items is very loose. They are there only because we have chosen to put them there. The basis for that choice may be a vague sense that they 'belong' in a certain area. The basis may also be one of 'provocation', because we want to see what happens if the items are put together (as in a stratal*).

'What does this cluster lead to?'

'Take this cluster forward.'

'What do you get from this stratal?'

'Progress this forward.'

We really also need a word for this bag of items that we are holding temporarily together.

The written punctuation mark is somewhat easier than the spoken reference to the cluster. The suggested mark is shown in Figure 21 overleaf. The mark is placed before the cluster to indicate both the nature of the cluster and a request to 'take it forward' to some outcome.

---

* See page 233.

Figure 21 (( ))

(( )) Shared work, part-time, more leisure, quality of life, unemployment, black economy.

(( )) Street crime, drug need, basic economic need, crime culture,
gangs, peer groups, role models, no escape, police, overcrowded
courts, deterrence.

The ordinary language device of 'What does this lead to?' is
probably adequate to convey the 'to' of water logic.

'What does this lead to?'

'Where do we go from this?'

'Take this forward.'

'What follows?'

'What comes next?'

For written language a simple arrow placed after the word
or phrase would suffice, as suggested in Figure 22.

Figure 22 $\longrightarrow$

Deciding where your taxes should go. →

Restriction of part of earnings to defined spending. →

Attention-directing is a key part of thinking. We usually
achieve this with a question. The CoRT thinking tools (CAF,
PMI, C&S, etc.) can also direct attention, as do the Six Hats.

'Direct your attention to …'

'Focus on …'

'Hold your attention on …'

The written Spanish language has the very sensible device of
putting the question mark at the beginning of the question. This
immediately allows the reader to know that a question is now
being posed. This is much more sensible than only indicating

at the end that it is a question. We could shift the question mark to the beginning of the question or we could create a new 'attention-directing' indicator as suggested in Figure 23.

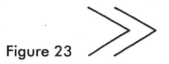

Figure 23

>> The check-in procedure at airports.
>> The congested air routes and air traffic control.
>> The future size of aircraft.
>> The layout of future terminals at airports.

You might want 'something to separate' the horses in one field from the sheep in another. That is a very broad concept. You might want a 'barrier' to effect the separation. You might want a 'fence'. You might want a 'wooden fence'. You might want a 'wooden fence with close vertical palings'. In this process we come down from a very broad concept to an almost detailed description of a fence. In thinking and in talking there would be value in being able to ask/indicate that there was a wish to go 'up' to a broader concept or 'down' from a broader concept to one that was more specific. It is not very easy to do this in ordinary language.

'Use a broader concept here.'

'Take this up to a broader concept.'

'Go down to a more specific concept.'

'What is the broad concept here?'

'Could you be more specific?'

At this point I am merely pinpointing a need for some elegant device rather than suggesting such a device.

With the written form we could use a simple arrow as suggested in Figure 24 overleaf. The arrow pointing upwards means 'going up' to a broader concept and the arrow pointing downwards means 'going down' to a more detailed concept.

Figure 24 ↑   ↓

↑ Sales tax.
↑ Passports.
↓ Distributed processing.
↓ Offshore banking.

I want to make clear that none of the forms and devices suggested here is essential to the skilful operation of parallel thinking. I have included them to indicate that we do not have to be complacent about what existing language can do for us. There is no reason to suppose that language has reached a stage of perfection and cannot be changed for the better. I have also intended this section to be a sort of test-model for complacency and change. It is very easy in looking at the suggestions to resist change because it is change. It is easy to say that you do not see the value or purpose of the device because you have not made an effort to look forward to see the effect. There is also the usual transition problem of introduction: 'No one else will understand what I am doing.' If it is within a closed group then this transitional problem is easily overcome. Where the Six Hats are now in use the terms have become part of the communication culture.

Do I expect the word 'popic' to catch on? Probably not, because, although it has a great convenience, the meaning is not immediately obvious. I do, however, expect the term 'parallel thinking' to catch on, because I know how easily it has done so when I have used it. Also the meaning is direct and simple. Finally, the term provides a needed contrast with the head-on clash of adversarial thinking. The term 'parallel thinking' directly implies cooperative thinking in parallel.

PARALLEL THINKING VS. WESTERN THINKING

At this point it may be useful to summarize the essential differences between traditional Western thinking (the Socratic method, the Gang of Three, etc.) and parallel thinking.

Traditional thinking is firmly based on 'judgement'. This is the key mental activity:

Is/is not.
True/false.
Either/or.
Fit/does not fit.
Right/wrong.
Proved/not proved.
What are we judging?

We set up 'true' definitions, categories, boxes, and we judge whether something fits into a box or not. We judge which box the matter fits into. We may seek to derive these boxes from experience, as Socrates sought to derive his true definitions of 'justice', etc., or we may decree these boxes, as in 'game truth' (we decide the rules of the game).

We set up either/or dichotomies and opposites in order to force a judgement choice. We seek to point out contradictions also to force a judgement choice or to prove another party wrong.

We also judge consistency, fit and the sufficiency of evidence for a statement.

Why are we doing all this?

We are doing it because we want to 'discover' the truth. We are interested in the truth of 'what is'. We believe that if you have the truth then all else is easy. It is a basic 'search idiom', like prospecting for gold. To help us in this search we use analysis and we collect information.

New ideas are supposed to be presented by evolution, by creative individuals or by an 'opposites' process of thesis/antithesis followed by synthesis. Once presented, the ideas are battered into useful shape by criticism. Judgement is always within the existing paradigm.

In parallel thinking the key idiom is 'design', not search. We seek to design a way forward. You need to design and construct a house. You do not 'discover' a house.

In parallel thinking, instead of the harsh accept/reject operation of judgement, there is 'possibility'. We accept possibilities even if they are contradictory and mutually exclusive. We lay them down alongside each other in parallel.

In parallel thinking, instead of adversarial argument in which one side tries to refute the propositions of the other side, there is parallel cooperative thinking in which all parties are looking in the same direction at any one moment. (There are frames for helping this, such as the Six Hats method.)

In parallel thinking, instead of hard-edged boxes and categories, there are flagpoles and spectra and overlap. Expressions like 'usually', 'by and large' and 'sometimes' are acceptable in place of the 'always', 'never', 'all' and 'none' of traditional judgement thinking. This arises from the use of 'possibly' instead of yes/no.

In parallel thinking there is an attempt to reconcile contradictions instead of choosing one and totally rejecting the other.

In parallel thinking there is a great emphasis on the direct creation of new ideas and new concepts. This process can be helped by the formal techniques of lateral thinking. It is not just a matter of waiting for ideas to emerge.

In parallel thinking there is as much emphasis on concepts as on information.

In parallel thinking we pay great attention to perception, because that is how we organize experience – as perceptions and concepts. Because we are dealing with perceptions, we can use the flow of 'water logic' rather than traditional 'rock logic'.

In parallel thinking a useful outcome is obtained by 'design' rather than by 'judgement'. From the field of parallel possibilities we design our way forward.

In parallel thinking we are concerned with action rather than with description. We are concerned with the values that arise from the 'truth' rather than only with the 'truth' itself.

We can now look at some of these points again in a direct contrast manner.

'What can be' vs. 'What is'.

Design vs. search.

Build vs. discover.

Create vs. repeat.

Constructive vs. destructive.

Action vs. description.

All these indicate a positive and constructive effort to bring something about. It is not a matter of discovering 'what is' but of designing a way forward. It may be a matter of creating new ideas rather than repeating the standard ones. It should be pointed out that Socrates was searching for the 'truth' in ethics, where the search method was probably appropriate. It is the application of that method to all areas that is the deficiency of Western thinking.

In parallel thinking a useful outcome is obtained by 'design' rather than by 'judgement'. From the field of parallel possibilities we design our way forward.

Possible vs. certain.

Acceptance vs. refutation.

Value vs. righteousness.

These indicate a broad view and a tolerance. Instead of the instant gatekeeper judgement of traditional thinking there is acceptance of all items as 'possibles'. Once the possibles have been laid alongside each other then the outcome is produced through the design process. Now the whole field can be seen. Now the whole system can be seen.

Windows vs. categories.

Flagpoles vs. boxes.

Spectrum vs. dichotomies.

Overlap vs. discrimination.

Soft edge vs. hard edge.

Reconcile vs. reject (contradictions).

All these indicate a softening of the rigid 'box' system that is at the heart of Western traditional thinking. This follows the replacement of judgement by the acceptance of 'possible'. Instead of forcing the world into an imposed order of boxes we can let information organize itself; if it does not, we can design a way forward.

Parallel vs. adversarial.

Laying alongside vs. gatekeeper judging.

Exploration vs. clash.

The practical operation of traditional thinking often involves argument, adversarial clash and dialectic. This is seen as essential to the thinking process. In parallel thinking dialectic is not essential. Instead there is the cooperative attempt to explore the subject thoroughly and to develop new perceptions and new concepts.

Perceptions vs. processing.

Subjective vs. objective.

'To' vs. 'is'.

Water logic vs. rock logic.

'What next' vs. 'what is'.

Flow vs. identity.

Self-organizing vs. externally organized.

The way we look at the world is determined in our minds. Our concepts and perceptions provide the frames through which we look at the world and with which we deal with the world. We seek to make these frames as valid as possible. When dealing with perception we need to use the water logic of flow, which relates to how one state of activity in the brain 'flows' to another. Our perceptions are already self-organizing. We seek to help, and change, that self-organizing process in order to produce better perceptions and concepts.

Ideas vs. information.

Creative vs. deductive.

Provocation vs. description.

Movement vs. judgement.

These indicate the emphasis on 'creating' new ideas and new possibilities. That has always been the basis of science and of progress. In creating new ideas you do not have to be 'right' at each step. You can use deliberate provocations and then move forward from these to useful new ideas. Valuable creative ideas will always be logical in hindsight but are not obtainable by logic in foresight, because of the asymmetric nature of patterning systems. Analysis of information will allow us to choose from among our standard ideas but will not create new ones. Information by itself is not enough. It is only concepts that give value to information.

Whole vs. part.

Non-linear vs. linear.

System vs. element.

You can only assess the contribution of an element to the whole system when you look at the whole system. Analysing out the parts and judging them will give a false impression. The 'acceptance' and 'possibility' of parallel thinking make it easier to look at the whole picture. Circumstances, contexts and interactions give value to the parts of the system.

Forward vs. backward.

Change vs. stability.

Challenge vs. defend.

In place of the defence of the existing state of affairs, there is an effort to move forward to make things better. Traditional thinking is poor at coping with change, because change is compared to what is and is rejected for as long as possible. In the 'design' idiom of parallel thinking we seek to move forward.

Wisdom vs. cleverness.

Plural vs. single.

Humility vs. arrogance.

These suggest the broad view that takes in the big picture. There is an acceptance of alternatives and different points of view. There is not the arrogance which springs from the 'one-truth' idiom (my truth).

In the parallel thinking system, points of difference are not mutually exclusive dichotomies. There is not the choice of one and the rejection of the other. Parallel thinking does not use such hard-edged boxes. The points of contrast between the two systems are like the ends of a spectrum. For example, judgement may be at one end and design at the other. Parallel thinking is then closer to the design end of the spectrum than is traditional thinking, which is very close to the judgement end.

For example, parallel thinking does use judgement in order to decide whether a 'designed' outcome is useful or valid. The difference is that judgement is used at this point, not as a way of getting the outcome. Similarly, parallel thinking is also concerned with stability, but this is the stability built out of useful change and not through the rejection of all change. Again, parallel thinking acknowledges the full value of information, but believes that information is not enough unless supplemented by concepts.

Sometimes the difference between parallel thinking and the Western thinking system is a matter of sharp contrast. Traditional adversarial argument is completely different from parallel exploration of a subject. The acceptance of possibilities is different from gatekeeper judgement. Green is a different colour from blue.

At other times it is a matter of tendency and emphasis. In parallel thinking there may be more emphasis on perception than in traditional thinking. There may be more emphasis on generating ideas than on judging them. We could say: 'This colour is more green than blue.'

It should by now be clear that there is a real and fundamental difference between parallel thinking and traditional Western thinking. There are huge differences of operation. There are huge differences in the basics: design vs. discovery; possibility vs. judgement, etc. To try to fit them into the same 'box' weakens the value of each thinking method and could only be achieved with a box labelled 'thinking'. It is also futile to point out that some element of each method occurs in the other. There is indeed some overlap, but the 'flagpoles' are far apart. There is some speculation in traditional thinking just as there is some judgement in parallel thinking. Aeroplanes and birds both fly; a mechanical ditch digger and a mole both make holes in the ground.

In one system we have judgement of the 'truth' as defined by categories we have set up.

In the other system we design forward from a field of parallel possibilities.

SUMMARY 2
THE FAILURE OF
WESTERN THINKING

It is now time to pull together the various points that have been made in the book regarding the 'failure' of Western thinking. We can look at this failure under three possible headings:

1. Western thinking has failed because it is suitable only for certain purposes and totally inadequate for other purposes.
2. Western thinking has failed because it is actually dangerous and forces us to look at the world in a harmful way.
3. Western thinking has failed because its complacency and its ability to defend itself have made it impossible to develop different thinking methods.

The Socratic method was designed for a very specific purpose. Following the subjectivity of the sophists, some of whom believed that personal perceptual truths were the only truths, Socrates set out to 'discover' the 'true definitions' of such things as 'justice'. He was concerned with putting ethics on to a firm basis so that the persuasive skills of the sophists could no longer sway society. Plato, with his strong fascist tendencies, developed the notion of 'ideal forms' which was imposed on the world by his thinking. Later, Aristotle (the third member of the Gang of Three) tightened up the system and showed its application to science. Throughout the ages this 'discovery-of-the-truth' idiom has been very attractive to philosophers, to religious thinkers and to scientists because it has been the basis of their employment.

But this idiom is totally inadequate when there is a need to construct, to build, to change and to design a way forward. You can discover gold, but you have to design and build a house. Applying standard ideas is no use if there is a need to develop new ideas. Where problems cannot be solved by identifying and removing the cause, there is a need to 'design a way forward'.

Our thinking habits and our education have placed all the emphasis on analysis and judgement. There has been no emphasis placed on design and creativity. Yet the present-day problems of the world are crying out for those skills.

The traditional thinking system has simply been inadequate on the 'generative', 'creative' and 'productive' side. This is because the traditional thinking system was not designed for such purposes at all. Neither Socrates nor Plato was to blame. You cannot blame the designers of a farm tractor if someone finds it not much use as a racing car. The fault lies with those who have failed to see the inadequacy of the system and who, to this day, seek to defend it as complete.

The traditional thinking system seeks to attack fault, to solve problems and to correct what is 'wrong'. Yet progress needs to come from challenging and rethinking concepts which have been 'right' in their time. Because we have come to accept such concepts as 'truths', we defend them vigorously and never see any value in challenging them. In any case, the system provides no means for challenging them.

There is no place for formal creativity in the traditional thinking system. Nor is there any place for 'design'. If you are seeking to discover the truth then you are not interested in 'creating truths'.

Of course, creativity has been permitted in the arts and to talented individuals, but it has never been accepted as a mainstream necessity. Yet we now know that there is a mathematical necessity for creativity in any self-organizing information system like the human brain. What are we going to do about it?

So traditional Western thinking has been inadequate in the creative and design side of thinking. That such thinking has taken place at all is due to individual energy, the possibility system (not the judgement system) and the search for the truth. This last element is indeed part of the traditional thinking system, and has been a good motivator in science, but in complex, non-linear systems design has now become more important than discovery.

We can now move on to the actual dangers of the traditional thinking system. From the 'search for the truth' and the harshness of the judgement system have come righteousness, arrogance and intolerance of plurality. When you have found the 'truth' you know that everyone else must be 'wrong'. Indeed you must show them that they are wrong, because this is one of the fundamental ways of proving that you are right. You set up a mutually exclusive dichotomy and then prove the other side wrong.

It would be unfair to claim that discrimination and racism arise from this judgement/box idiom of Western thinking, because other cultures show the same tendency from time to time. But it could be said that Western thinking has reinforced and legitimized these nasty habits of mind.

The need for dialectic clash in order to get at the truth has led directly to the verbal conflict of adversarial argument. Once again this legitimizes and reinforces the nasty combative habit of humans when they want to get their own way. In practice this argument habit is extraordinarily inefficient and ineffective. It allows the operation of personal power politics and never makes full use of the intellectual talent available. It puts matters into the 'us-and-them' mode. It is only when one has seen the effectiveness of parallel thinking (for example within the Six Hats framework) that the sheer incompetence of the argument method becomes obvious.

Western thinking is failing because its complacent arrogance prevents it from seeing the extent of its failure.

Because criticism is so very easy (just choose a frame different from the one offered), it has become a dominating habit of even intelligent people. There is a ridiculous belief that it is enough to get rid of the 'bad things' and what will be left are good things. Today's experience all over the world shows that getting rid of the bad things only results in chaos. There may no longer be any person or party to blame, but that is the only gain.

The elevation of the 'critical intelligence' to the highest level of human endeavour has probably been the single greatest mistake of Western intellectual development. Yet that is still the basis of our culture and our universities. That is danger indeed. Think of all that wasted intellectual talent which might have been harnessed to creative and constructive effort.

In times of total stability the critical intelligence might have been necessary to prevent any change and to keep things on the agreed course. But we are so very poor at dealing with change because we still hold that dangerous belief.

We now come to the third leg of the 'failure' of Western thinking. This is complacency. The Gang of Three really set up a belief system which forces us to look at the world in a way which confirms that belief system. It is a system that is very good at attack and defence on its own terms. It is like a Frenchman in France telling you that you must speak French if you are in France.

For historic reasons the thinking of the Gang of Three was very welcome at the Renaissance, because it replaced dogma and scripture with logic and reason. Both the humanists and the

Church thinkers eagerly embraced this wonderful new thinking (which it was at the time). So this particular system of thinking captured the heights of Western intellectual culture and has remained there ever since, because of its ability to defend itself with its own rules and to intimidate anyone who dares question its excellence.

Horrific as it may seem, there are people today who seriously believe that it is enough to teach 'critical thinking' in schools. This traditional type of judgement thinking has a high value but completely leaves out the constructive, productive, creative and 'operacy' side of thinking which is so desperately needed in society.

So the very existence of traditional Western thinking has meant that all educated people were brought up to believe in the sufficiency of analysis and debate. That is the only way they can think, and therefore they believe it to be the only possible way to think. But is it?

Because this traditional method seems so excellent in the particular universe of education (for analysing and commenting on what is put in front of you), people come to believe in its excellence. We have therefore made no effort to develop other methods of thinking. The intellectual 'guardians' of society (in the fascist Platonic sense) set as a method for everyone what happens to suit their own analytical purposes. Those who need to be constructive in society and those who wish to be constructive in society are treated as if they do not think and do not need to think. The constructive and creative side of thinking has been neglected because it is of less use to academics. Just as Chinese civilization was sterilized by reverence for its academics, so Western civilization is being held back by the notion that analysis and description are sufficient thinking skills.

We are all so entrained in the traditional Western way of thinking that it is difficult to stand back to look at its virtues, its peculiarities, its limitations and its arrogance. That it should be arrogant defines it as a belief system.

It is only by comparison with an alternative approach to thinking, as in parallel thinking, that we can come to see more clearly the nature of the Western thinking process that has so pre-empted our thinking about thinking.

I suspect that in the future computer software will allow us to use self-organizing field effects which will force us beyond the step-by-step propositional thinking to which we have been hitherto limited.

My own entry into the subject of thinking came directly from my work in medicine with the more complicated interactive systems (glands, kidneys, respiration, circulation) and the need to develop concepts of self-organizing information systems. This led to the consideration of behaviour in neural networks (see my book *The Mechanism of Mind*). From that came my interest in creative thinking and the development of the processes of lateral thinking. This led on to the importance of perceptions and concepts, and eventually to a realization that traditional thinking was not as complete and not as perfect as I had believed.

Western thinking has always assumed a particular information universe, just as Euclid assumed a plane surface for his geometry. If we move into self-organizing information universes then traditional thinking can be seen as only one particular thinking method.

So Western thinking is failing because it is not designed to deal with a changing world. It is failing because it is inadequate to deal with change, because it does not offer creative, constructive and design energy. It is failing because it suggests dangerous judgements and discriminations which tend to make things worse (as in legislative chambers and politics). It is failing because its complacent arrogance prevents it from seeing the extent of its failure.

ACTION EPILOGUE

This section need be read only by those people who, having come to the end of the book, ask: 'So what do we do about it?'

Since the purpose of parallel thinking is to design an outcome, it is only appropriate that those who seek an outcome from this book should have the opportunity to consider some suggestions.

In general, I think we should pay much more attention to the principles of parallel thinking. We need to rid ourselves of the obsession that criticism is enough. We need to do very much more about design, constructive thinking and creative thinking. It is no longer enough to suppose that these things are 'just going to happen'. We need to realize that we need ideas as much as we need information.

I am often asked by radio interviewers to tell listeners what they can do about their thinking if they do not want to buy a book or go on a course. This is rather like asking what you can do about eating if you do not want to buy food and do not want to go to a restaurant. If we really want to change our thinking habits then we do need to do some things. A slight change in attitude will not have much effect.

I would like to see 'thinking' taught as a specific subject in all schools. Thinking should also be infused into other subject areas, but it does benefit from being the centre of attention in specific 'thinking lessons'. Many schools and some countries have been doing this for some time already. It is not enough that there should be the old-fashioned critical thinking, which is so lacking in the creative and constructive aspects of thinking. There is a need for 'operacy' and the skills of doing. Analysis and judgement are not sufficient.

It is no longer excuse enough to say that it cannot be done or that there are no practical ways of teaching thinking. The *CoRT Thinking Lessons* have now been in use for many years in many countries with many different cultures. The students respond to them very well. The Six Hats method for teaching structured parallel thinking is also now becoming more widely used in schools. So there are practical things that can be done, and experience with these. To claim that these things cannot be done is like proving that cheese does not exist. It does.

At all levels in education I would like much more attention paid to the 'design' side of thinking. We need to supplement the usual focus on analysis with an equal emphasis on design. How do you bring things about? How do you make things happen? How do you create new ideas? We need to be specific about teaching the skills and habit of design. This is 'design' in its broadest sense and not just buildings and machines. We need to consider complex interactive systems and how we can design within such frameworks. This should apply in all subject areas, so that even those who have less need to use design will know what it is about and why judgement alone is not sufficient.

Creativity and the design process and parallel thinking itself are only ways of achieving constructive results.

We need to pay attention to 'serious creativity'. Creativity is no longer a matter of messing around and hoping that ideas will emerge. Creativity is much more than taking off your tie, feeling liberated and brainstorming. Such processes are weak and old-fashioned. There are formal techniques, such as those of lateral thinking, which can be applied as deliberately as we might use a mathematical procedure. All students in whatever subject area should be given the chance to develop such skills. We must get away from the belief that creativity is the business of only a few talented geniuses.

I would almost like to see governments taking 'design' seriously enough to have a Department or Ministry for New Ideas. Such a department would seek to encourage and collect emerging ideas. Such a department would set up teams to develop new ideas on specific issues.

I would like to see the United Nations set up a formal Office of Creativity. This would provide a framework for focusing design thinking on issues and problems. Such an office would also provide a platform for the bringing forward of new ideas which might be too politically sensitive to be ascribed to one country or another.

I would like to see International Creative Commissions set up to do some new thinking and some design thinking around specified subjects: healthcare, ecology, employment, etc.

Businesses are already starting to use the Six Hats method of parallel thinking because they find it so much more powerful and productive than traditional argument. All organizations should seek to put this simple procedure into their operating culture.

I would like to see society having the courage to challenge and rethink some of our most basic concepts in economics, in education, in government and elsewhere. There is good reason to believe that existing concepts have reached the end of their useful life.

I would like to see an international centre set up which would focus directly on the improvement of thinking methods. Part of the work of such a centre would be training people to train others. Part would be the development of better thinking tools and processes. Part would be organizing Creative

Commissions to rethink standard concepts and methods. Such a centre could become the focus for the new culture of thinking.

Throughout, the final emphasis should be on constructive thinking. Creativity and the design process and parallel thinking itself are only ways of achieving constructive results.

It is no longer enough to talk about the top of the mountain. It is no longer enough to talk about 'peace' or a 'pollution-free world'. There is a need to develop climbing techniques if we are going to get to the top of the mountain.

We do not have to throw out the traditional system of thinking. But we need to be aware of its dangers. We need to note where it is excellent and where it is inadequate. We need to combine the generative processes of parallel thinking with the judgement processes of critical thinking.

Above all we need the courage to question whether the thinking system which we have held so dear for 2,500 years is really going to be adequate to guide us over the next 100 years. Being defensive and complacent about our thinking methods is almost as bad as considering that all this is someone else's business.

INDEX